Beginning iOS AR Game Development

Developing Augmented Reality Apps with Unity and C#

Allan Fowler

Apress®

Beginning iOS AR Game Development: Developing Augmented Reality Apps with Unity and C#

Allan Fowler
Marietta, GA, USA

ISBN-13 (pbk): 978-1-4842-3617-8   ISBN-13 (electronic): 978-1-4842-3618-5
https://doi.org/10.1007/978-1-4842-3618-5

Library of Congress Control Number: 2018964038

Managing Director, Apress Media LLC: Welmoed Spahr
Acquisitions Editor: Aaron Black
Development Editor: James Markham
Coordinating Editor: Jessica Vakili

Cover image designed by Freepik (www.freepik.com)

Distributed to the book trade worldwide by Springer Science+Business Media New York, 233 Spring Street, 6th Floor, New York, NY 10013. Phone 1-800-SPRINGER, fax (201) 348-4505, e-mail orders-ny@springer-sbm.com, or visit www.springeronline.com. Apress Media, LLC is a California LLC and the sole member (owner) is Springer Science + Business Media Finance Inc (SSBM Finance Inc). SSBM Finance Inc is a **Delaware** corporation.

For information on translations, please e-mail rights@apress.com, or visit http://www.apress.com/rights-permissions.

Apress titles may be purchased in bulk for academic, corporate, or promotional use. eBook versions and licenses are also available for most titles. For more information, reference our Print and eBook Bulk Sales web page at http://www.apress.com/bulk-sales.

Any source code or other supplementary material referenced by the author in this book is available to readers on GitHub via the book's product page, located at www.apress.com/978-1-4842-3617-8. For more detailed information, please visit http://www.apress.com/source-code.

Printed on acid-free paper

For Hao, Ciaran, & Annah - kia kaha, kia aroha, kia mana

Table of Contents

About the Author

Dr. Allan Fowler is a Professor in Game Design at Kennesaw State University. Fowler lives in Atlanta, GA. Fowler is a published author, game designer, and dedicated educator. Apart from looking after his two children, in his spare time he makes games and practices martial arts and is a keen amateur photographer. Dr. Fowler holds a fifth degree black belt in Shorin-Ryu karate and has competed in State and International karate tournaments.

About the Technical Reviewer

Felipe Laso is a Senior Systems Engineer working at Lextech Global Services. He's also an aspiring game designer/programmer. You can follow him on Twitter as @iFeliLM or on his blog.

CHAPTER 1

Introduction

In this book, we are going to learn how to create an Augmented Reality
(or AR) Game using the game development software from Unity (Unity3D
2018 or, more commonly, Unity). In this chapter, we will go through the
process of downloading and installing Unity and learn about some of the
tools that Unity provides. We will also install an existing AR project from the
Unity Asset Store and explore some of the features of this game. In Chapter 2,
we will install the ARKit and provide an overview of the Unity user interface.
In Chapter 3, we will start using the Unity ARKit and use some of the key
functions. I will also provide a basic overview of visual inertial odometry and
what this means for creating AR projects. We will make a basic scene to use
and test Unity ARKit. In Chapter 4, we will use some of the more advanced
functions in Unity ARKit such as hit testing and lighting an AR scene. Finally,
in Chapter 5, we will put this all together and make an AR game using the
Unity ARKit.

   This book has been written for a beginner that has no prior experience
using Unity or making games. The chapters have been prepared in a
sequence to help learn each step. However, if you are reading this book
and already know about Unity or making games, then feel free to skip
whatever chapters you feel you already know.

© Allan Fowler 2019
A. Fowler, *Beginning iOS AR Game Development*,
https://doi.org/10.1007/978-1-4842-3618-5_1

Unity3D

The Unity game engine is a cross-platform game development tool for creating both 2D and 3D games. The term cross-platform can mean different things to different people. As Unity can be used on macOS, Windows, or Linux, this could be considered a cross-platform development tool. However, as Unity can be used to develop games for a games console, personal computer, web browser, mobile devices, VR systems, etc., this could also be why Unity is considered a cross-platform development tool.

Unity can be used to create 3D games, that is, the game looks like it operates in a 3D space (it has an X, Y, **and** a Z). Unity can also be used to create 2D games. More recently, Unity has been used to create VR and AR games or simulations.

In this book, we will use the latest version of Unity, which is currently 2018.1. However, like most software (and a lot of hardware), Unity is constantly introducing new features, functionality, and by the time this book has been printed, there may be a more current version of Unity available. When Unity makes a minor change to their software, they will typically add a number (like 2018.1.1). When the update is a bit more substantial, then the version number will change (like 2018.2). When Unity typically make a major change, then the version number will change completely (Unity 1, 2, 3, 4, 5). In July 2017, Unity changed the version numbering system to the year of release (2017 and now 2018).

Unity Requirements

Before you start learning to make games, you will need to download Unity and install it on your Mac. Although it is possible to make games for iOS devices with Unity installed on a Windows Personal Computer, you will need to use a piece of software called Xcode to port the Unity code so it can run on a Mac or iOS device. Currently, Xcode is only available on a Mac. So, if you have a Windows PC, then at some stage you will need to use a Mac to port the game. Throughout this book, I will use a Mac; if you are using a Windows PC, then many of the instructions or directions may not apply to you.

Preparing Your Mac

For iOS development using Unity, you will need a Mac running the Lion or Mountain Lion of Mac OS X 10.9 or higher and Xcode 7.0 or higher. Unity 2018 may still run on some older systems, but you will need the latest version of Xcode, which, as noted, is required for iOS development. The latest version of Xcode typically supports the more recent versions of iOS. At the time of writing, the current version of Xcode is version 9, which is what I'll be using throughout this book.

Getting Registered

I highly recommend checking out the Apple Developer website (`https://developer.apple.com/`) and registering as an iOS developer. Although it is not an absolute requirement of this book, if you want to publish games on the App Store, then you will need to be a registered Apple Developer. The process of registering as an Apple Developer can take a while, especially if you are registering a company. The first step is registering as an Apple Developer (which is currently free), then once you are registered, the next step is registering as an iOS developer (which is currently $99 per year).

Download Xcode

You won't need Xcode until much later in the book, but it would be worth downloading and installing Xcode. You can find the latest version of Xcode on the Apple Developer website (`https://developer.apple.com/`).

Download Unity

Now would be a great time to install Unity. Go to the Unity website at `https://unity3d.com` and then select Get Unity or type in `https://store.unity.com/`. On this page, you will find the latest release of Unity (at the time of writing, 2018.1). You can also find previous releases of Unity on the Unity website.

While there is only a single Unity application, you can subscribe to different licensing options, depending on your needs and the size of your company (if you have one). The three licensing options are currently Personal, Plus, and Pro. To start the download process, click on the button of the subscription option that suits your needs (at the time of writing, this will be either Try Personal, Get Plus, or Go Pro). The file is about 1GB, so it may take a while to download. While you're waiting, and you are on the

Unity website, take some time to check out some of the games and demos that have been published, the community site, and the user forum. These will be very useful throughout the development of games using Unity.

Install Unity

The file you downloaded from Unity is a Download Installer, which at the time of writing is named UnityDownloadAssistant.

Running the Download Assistant

When the UnityDownloadAssistant file has been downloaded, double-click the file to run the Unity Download Assistant. Double-click the Unity Download Assistant icon to start installing Unity (Figure 1-1).

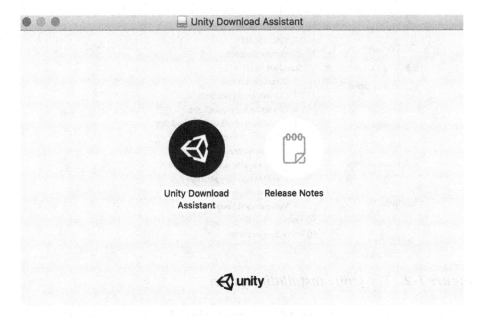

Figure 1-1. The Unity Download Assistant

The installer will process through the installation cycle, and when this is complete, a Unity folder will be placed in the Applications folder (unless you selected a different location). If you have previous versions of Unity installed, an installation of a new version may replace the previous version. I recommend renaming the folder of the previous version before installing the new version (for example, Unity2017). This way you can still use both versions of Unity.

The Unity installation folder contains the Unity application and several support folders and applications (Figure 1-2).

Figure 1-2. *The Unity installation folder*

One of the most important files in the Unity folder is the Unity application, which will provide the tools used to create and test your games. This application is sometimes referred to as the Unity Editor, which is different from another application, the Unity Runtime Engine (also known as the Unity Player). The Unity Runtime Engine is integrated into the final builds, which will enable the game to be played on the target hardware. When I refer to Unity, I am usually referring to the Unity Editor. I sometimes will refer to the company Unity technologies as Unity. But hopefully, the context will be clear.

The Documentation folder contains the User Manual, Component Reference, and the Script Reference documents. These are also available on the Unity website (select the Learn link). All of these files are HTML documents and can be opened in a web browser from the Unity Help menu system, or they can be opened directly by double-clicking the file.

The Standard Assets folder contains several files with the .unityPackage file extension. These are Unity package files that contain collections of Unity assets, which can be imported into Unity. It is also possible to create your own Standard Assets and export these assets to a package file.

There is also the Unity Bug Reporter Application. This application is typically run directly from within the Unity Editor using the Report a Bug function. However, this application run directly from the Unity installation folder.

If you downloaded the Example Project with the Unity installation, be sure to open this in Unity. If you did not download this at installation, it still could be downloaded at any time.

Welcome

After Unity has finished installing (and be prepared for it to take a while), the Unity editor welcome screen will appear with the Unity Hello! Window (Figure 1-3). The Unity Hello! Window is where you sign into your Unity account (if you have one). If you don't have a Unity account, select the create one link. If you are not currently connected to the Internet, you can work offline by selecting the Work offline button.

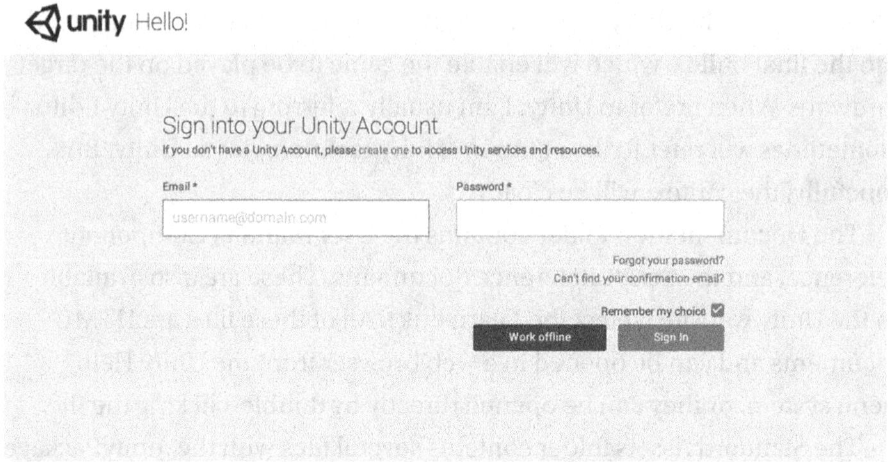

Figure 1-3. *The Unity Hello! screen*

The Unity Hello! window will appear when you start up Unity (Figure 1-3). I highly recommend creating a Unity account, if you haven't already created one.

After signing in for the first time, you will see the License management screen. If you have paid for the licensed version of Unity, enter your license serial number in the dialog box. If you want to use the free version of Unity, select the Unity Personal radio button (Figure 1-4).

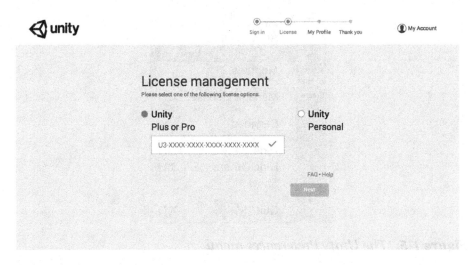

Figure 1-4. *The Unity license management screen*

Setting Up Unity

Before we get into making a game with Unity, this is a good time to review some of the options and administrative features of Unity.

Changing Skins (Pro Version)

If you have purchased a Pro license of Unity, you will be able to choose between a light or dark skin. If you are using the free version of Unity, you will only see the Light Skin.

As most beginner game developers use the free version of Unity, I will use the light skin for screenshots. The light skin also produces better screenshots for the paperback version of this book. If you have the Pro version and want to change the skin, select Preferences in the Unity menu (Figure 1-5).

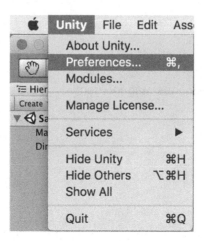

Figure 1-5. *The Unity Preferences menu*

With the Preferences menu open, you can change the skin from Dark to Light or Light to Dark (Figure 1-6). If you are using Unity Personal edition, you're stuck with the Light skin.

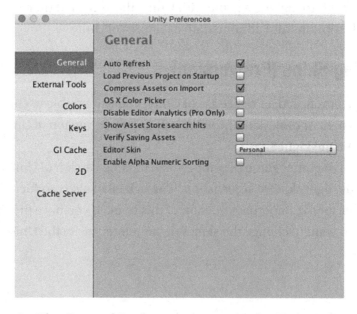

Figure 1-6. *The General Preferences menu in the Unity Editor*

While you have the General Preferences menu open, I would recommend making sure the Load Previous Project on Startup option is deselected. This will ensure that Unity loads the project selection dialog at startup. This will make sure you avoid updating the wrong version of the project or update the version of Unity you are using before you are ready.

Reporting Problems

If you continue to use Unity for several years, you will encounter some bugs (both real and imagined). I have been using Unity since version 1.6 and have encountered several bugs with Unity. Software bugs are not unique to Unity. A game development engine is a complex piece of software and Unity certainly appreciates and values bug reports. If the bugs aren't reported, then it's difficult for Unity to fix them. The Unity Bug Reporter application provides this feature. As noted earlier, the Report a Bug Reporter is available in the Unity installation folder and is available from the Help menu in the Unity Editor (Figure 1-7).

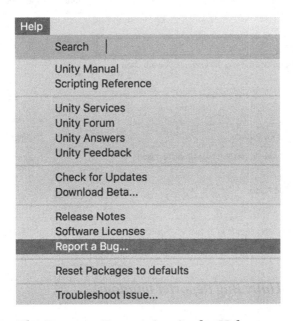

Figure 1-7. *The Report a Bug option in the Help menu*

Selecting the Report, a Bug option on the help menu or double-clicking the Report a Bug application in the Unity installation folder opens the Unity Report a Bug application (Figure 1-8). The application provides menu options and dialog boxes for the user to specify what the problem is related to, how often the problem happens, the title of the bug, the details of the bug, and an option to attach any relevant files that will help fix the bug. The Unity Bug Reporter requires the user to specify an email address so that the team at Unity can respond to the bug report.

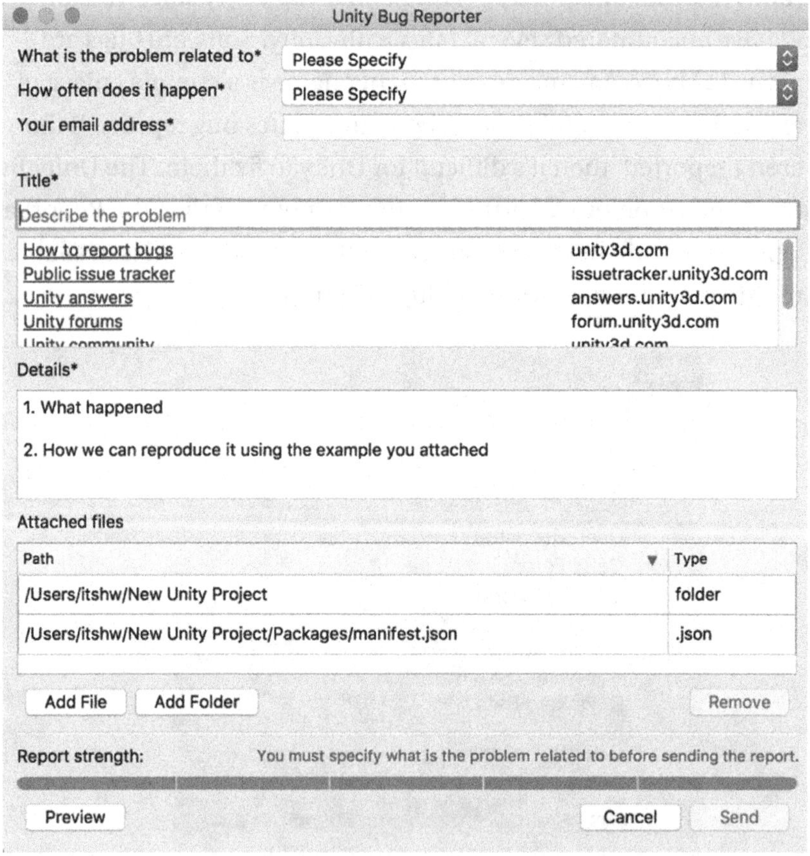

Figure 1-8. *The Unity Bug Reporter window*

iOS Development Requirements

Earlier in this chapter, I suggested that it would be a good idea to download Xcode and register for the Apple Developer Program. If you have not down this already, now would be a good time to stop and do this.

The hardware and software requirements for iOS development and details about the Apple Developer Program are listed on Apple's Developer support page (`https://developer.apple.com/`). You can also find the requirements and download page for Xcode at `https://developer.apple.com/Xcode/`.

The Unity Website

As Unity Technologies has increased the features and functionally of Unity, so has the also increased in breadth and depth of content. There is a lot of information on this website, but I would recommend looking at the FAQ section (`https://unity3d.com/unity/faq`). There are also some great tutorials, documentation, and videos that will help you learn to create games in Unity (`https://unity3d.com/unity/faq`).

The Unity Community

In the Help menu, there are links to the official Unity community sites. This includes the official Unity Forum (`https://forum.unity.com`), which is moderated by Unity staff. This is a great resource for any game developer. Also on this menu is a link to Unity Answers, which uses a Stack Exchange format and includes some control (or moderation) of the questions and answers.

The Unity feedback site (`https://feedback.unity3d.com`) enables developers to request and vote on possible future features.

Welcome to Unity.

CHAPTER 2

Getting Started

Hopefully, you might already have a good idea of what Augmented Reality (or AR) is. As there is some confusion about the difference between the terms Virtual Reality (or VR), Augmented Reality, and Mixed Reality, I thought it might be worth trying to clarify what I mean by AR in this book.

Virtual Reality (VR) is a computer-generated environment that simulates experience through senses and perception. Unlike a traditional computer system, VR systems place the user inside an experience. Instead of viewing a screen in front of them, users are immersed and able to interact with 3D worlds.

Now, let's look at Augmented Reality (AR). The general consensus is that AR is defined as a direct live view of a real-world environment whose elements are "augmented" by computer-generated information. The key difference between VR and AR is that AR includes a **live view** of the real environment. VR systems typically do not include a live view of the real environment. The VR headsets are fully enclosed, and the display is fully computer generated.

Mixed Reality (MR, although the acronym is rarely used), is a term that has mostly been used by Microsoft to differentiate their HoloLens. I feel that Mixed Reality is another form of AR. However, there is still some debate about this. When I asked my good friends at Microsoft, they felt that Mixed Reality is somewhere between AR and VR and fully integrates digital objects into your world, making it look as if they are really there.

© Allan Fowler 2019
A. Fowler, *Beginning iOS AR Game Development*,
https://doi.org/10.1007/978-1-4842-3618-5_2

It might surprise you that the terms VR and AR have been around for many years. While there is considerable debate about the first use of the term VR (mostly due to an agreed definition on the term), there is some general consensus that the term was first used around the 1950s where authors referred to fully immersive systems or environments. Throughout the U.S. Military and NASA, aircraft manufacturers used AR systems for training, research, and development. However, it was not until 2016 that we saw the first commercially available consumer AR system, the Oculus Rift. The Occulus Rift was manufactured by Oculus VR (which was eventually bought out by Facebook for $2,000,000,000).

References to AR have also been made for many years. The difficulty with agreeing as to then the first reference to AR was made is also due to an agreed definition of what is AR. In 1989, George Douglas wrote about a computer-driven astronomical telescope guidance and control system with a superimposed star field and celestial coordinate graphics display that appears to be the first AR system.

More recently, there have been several interesting developments in AR. Although there were some proprietary systems, the first most notable development was the introduction of Pokémon Go for Android and iOS phones. Using the geolocation capabilities and the integrated camera of the phone, users were able to see a virtual object appear on the screen to be in the real world.

In this book, I am going to focus on developing an AR game for iOS. I have chosen iOS for a number of reasons. First, there are a lot of devices that use iOS. More importantly, Apple is investing in AR development in both hardware and software. With iOS 11, Apple included the ARKit. ARKit makes it easy for us to create AR games and simulations that put virtual objects into the user's environment. Through combining information from the devices' motion sensors with data from its cameras, ARKit can help an iPhone or iPad analyze the surroundings. Apple also beefed up the capability of the cameras in both the iPhone 8 and iPhone X. The cameras in the iPhone 8 and iPhone X have been designed for shooting in low light and at 60-fps video. The dual optical image stabilization on iPhone X and improved optical image stabilization on the iPhone 8 also provide improved visual clarity. These hardware and software features help make the game appear more naturally in the user's environment. Apple is also investing heavily in improving the AR capabilities of their future iPhones and iPads.

Unity recently introduced the Unity ARKit in the Unity Store. This makes it a lot easier for us to make AR games for iOS. Therefore, throughout this book, I will be using the Unity ARKit. So now would be a good time to install the latest version of the Unity ARKit. The minimum requirements for the Unity ARKit are the following:

> iOS device that supports ARKit and has the latest version of iOS 11.3 or higher.

> Mac with macOS 10.13 (High Sierra) or higher.

> Unity version 2017.1 or higher.

> The latest version of XCode 9.3 (or higher) from the Apple Developer website (requires macOS 10.13).

Now that you have Unity installed, it's time to get acquainted with the various elements of the Unity ARKit that we will use to make and test our game. While we explore the different components of the Unity ARKit, I will discuss some of the technical principles of developing AR games. As this is an introductory book, I won't go too deep into the technical details and try to keep this relatively high level. My editor is asking me for recommendations on additional AR books, so I might keep the more advanced or technical content for the second book on AR.

Now let's start Unity and create a new project.

When you start Unity, you will see the Projects screen (Figure 2-1).

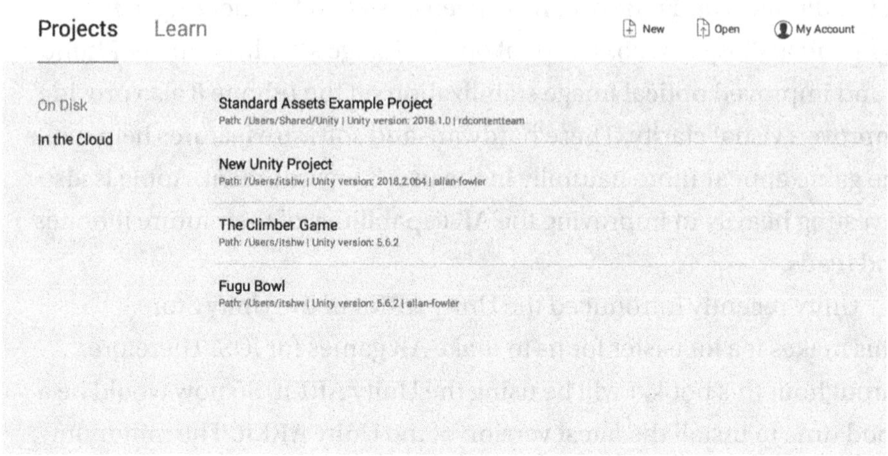

Projects   Learn   New   Open   My Account

On Disk   **Standard Assets Example Project**
                 Path: /Users/Shared/Unity | Unity version: 2018.1.0 | rdcontentteam
In the Cloud
                 New Unity Project
                 Path: /Users/itshw | Unity version: 2018.2.0b4 | allan-fowler

                 The Climber Game
                 Path: /Users/itshw | Unity version: 5.6.2

                 Fugu Bowl
                 Path: /Users/itshw | Unity version: 5.6.2 | allan-fowler

Figure 2-1. *The Unity Projects Screen*

Select the New icon on the top right of the screen. This will open
the Unity New Project screen (Figure 2-2). In the dialog boxes, type the
Project name in, set the location of the Unity file, type in the name of your
organization, and set the Template to 3D.

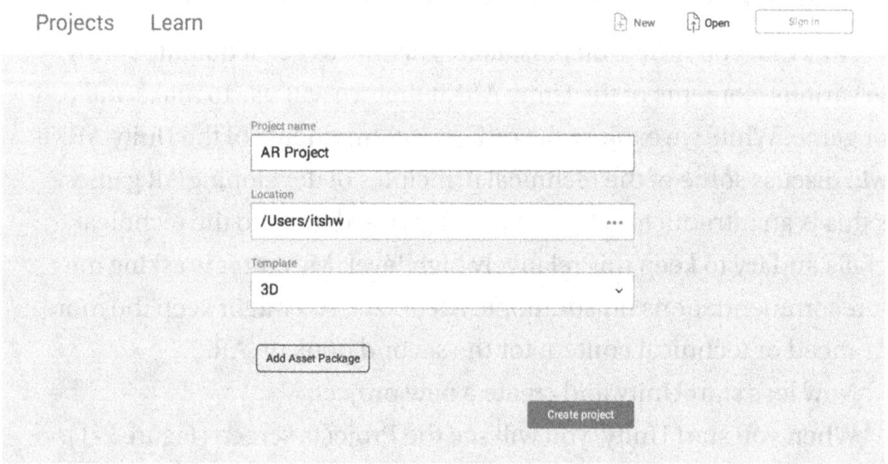

Projects   Learn   New   Open   Sign in

Project name

AR Project

Location

/Users/itshw   ...

Template

3D   ⌄

Add Asset Package

Create project

Figure 2-2. *The Unity New Project Screen*

In the dialog boxes of the Unity New Project screen, enter in the name of the project, select where you want to save this file, and select the Create project icon (Figure 2-2). I have chosen AR project as the file name and selected the Users folder on the hard drive.

Now Unity will open with a blank Unity project (Figure 2-3).

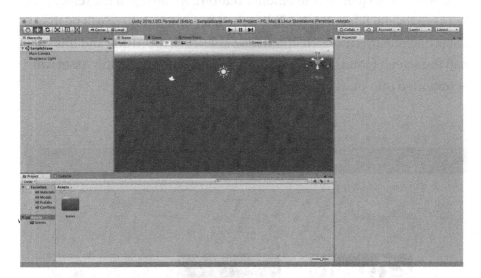

Figure 2-3. *A blank Unity projects screen*

Installing Unity ARKit

Now would be a great time to install the Unity ARKit. To install the Unity ARKit from the Unity Store, you will need to access the Unity Asset Store. The Unity Asset Store can be accessed a number of ways. In the main window of the Unity screen, there is an Asset Store tab, and this will bring up the Asset Store Window. This window can also be accessed by using the Command button and 9 (⌘+9). To download resources from the Asset Store, you will need to register with Unity to create a Unity ID. When you have created a Unity ID, in the Unity Asset Store window, there is a search bar. Type in the search bar ARKit, and this will bring up a list of files that

meet this search criterion (Figure 2-4). The default window settings in
Unity will show the Unity Store window minimized; to view the Asset Store
in Full-Screen mode, there is a drop-down menu on the top-right side of
the screen. Select this and click with the left mouse button. This will show
the screen options, Reload, Maximize, Close Tab, and Add Tab. Select the
maximize option (click the left mouse button). At the top of the screen,
there are several filter options. Below the filter options, there will be the
assets that meet your search criteria. Double-click the ARKit, and this will
load the screen for this asset. Select the import button, and this Asset will
be imported into Unity (Figure 2-5).

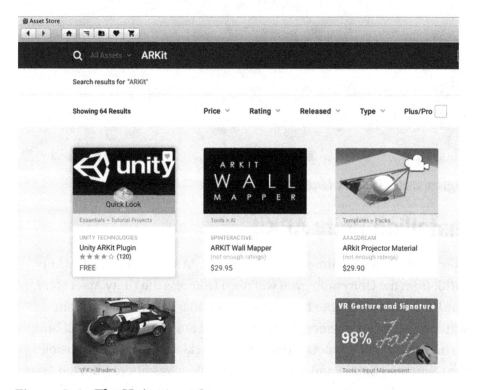

Figure 2-4. *The Unity Asset Store*

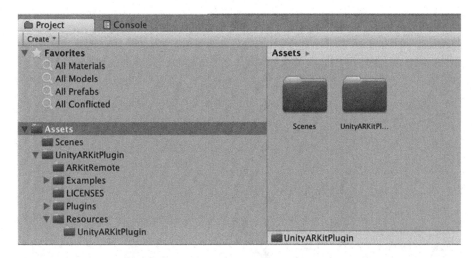

Figure 2-5. Unity Project Folder with the ARKit in the scene folder

The Editor Layout

Now would be a good time to take a closer look at the layout of the Unity Editor. The main window is divided into panels. The default displayed view (factory Settings) for an area is selected by clicking the view's tab. Views can be added, moved, removed, and resized, and the Editor supports switching among layouts, so a layout essentially is a specific arrangement of views. For example, the default layout of the main window (Figure 2-6) has an area containing a Scene View (Figure 2-7) and a Game View (Figure 2-8).

21

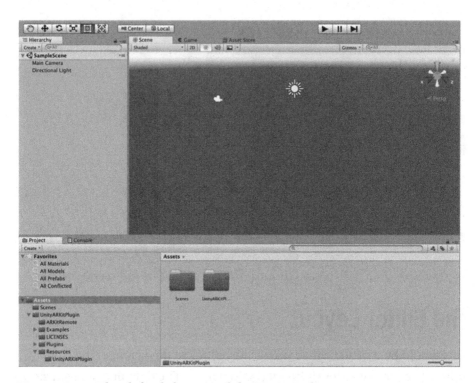

Figure 2-6. *The default layout of the Unity Editor*

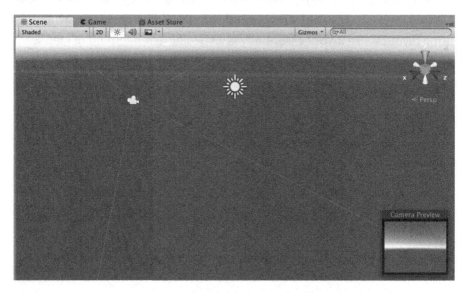

Figure 2-7. *The Scene View selected in a multitabbed area*

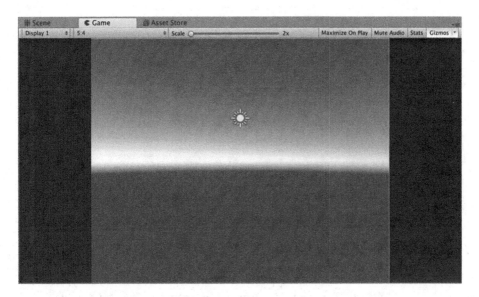

Figure 2-8. *The Game View selected in a multitabbed area*

Preset Layouts

The default layout is just one of several preset layouts. Alternate layouts can be selected from the menu in the top-right corner of the main window (Figure 2-9). Unity also enables us to create our own layout. In Figure 2-9, you will see that my menu has a Mobile Game Config. This is my custom Layout that I created for when I create Mobile Games. Check out the various Layouts on your menu. Figures 2-6 through 2-7 show the resulting layouts.

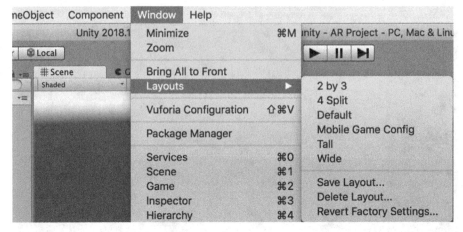

Figure 2-9. *The Layout menu*

I'll describe the individual types of views in more detail shortly, but for now, note that the 2-by-3 layout (Figure 2-10) is an example of a layout where the Scene View and Game View are in separate areas instead of sharing the same one. The 4-split layout (Figure 2-11) has four instances of the Scene View, demonstrating that a layout is not restricted to one of each type of view. The Tall Layout (Figure 2-12) provides a Portrait Scene View. The Wide Layout (Figure 2-13) provides a landscape Scene View.

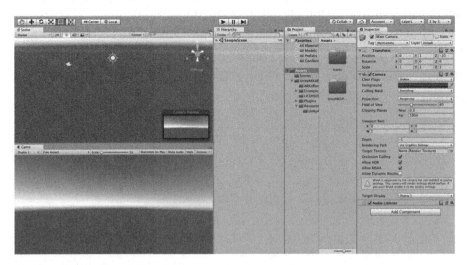

Figure 2-10. *The 2-by-3 layout*

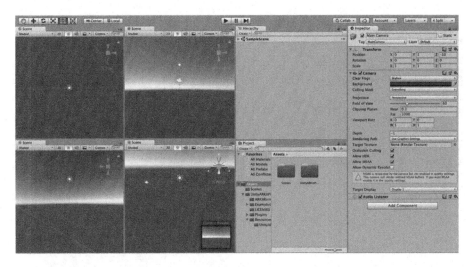

Figure 2-11. *The 4-split layout*

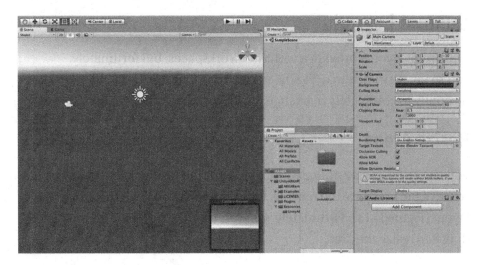

Figure 2-12. *The Tall layout*

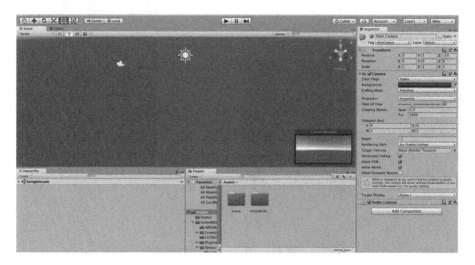

Figure 2-13.   *The Wide layout*

Custom Layouts

The preset layouts provide a variety of workspaces, but fortunately, you're not restricted to using them exactly as they are. Unity provides the flexibility to completely rearrange the Editor window as you like.

Resize Areas

For starters, you may notice while trying out the various preset layouts that some of the areas are too narrow, for example, in the left panel of the Wide layout (Figure 2-13). Fortunately, you can click the border of an area and drag it to resize the area.

Move Views

Even cooler, you can move views around. Dragging the tab of a view into another tab region will move the view there. And dragging the tab into a "docking" area will create a new area. For example, start with the Default

layout, and drag the Inspector tab to the right of the Hierarchy tab. Now
the Inspector View shares the same area as the Hierarchy View. The result
should look like Figure 2-14.

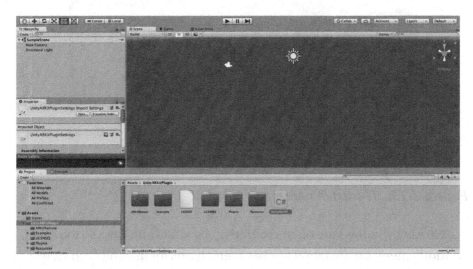

Figure 2-14. *Workspace customized with views moved*

Detach Views

You can even drag a view outside the Editor window so that it resides in
its own "floating" window, which can be treated just like any other area.
Drag the Scene tab outside the Editor, so it resides in a floating window,
and then drag the Game tab into its tab region. The result should look like
Figure 2-15. Likewise, dragging a tab into a docking region of the floating
window will add another area to the window.

Tip   I like to detach the Game View into a floating window, since I
normally don't need to see it while I'm working in the Editor until I
click Play, and this allows me to maximize the Game View to fill up to
the entire screen. I also like working with more than one monitor. This
way, I can maximize my screen space.

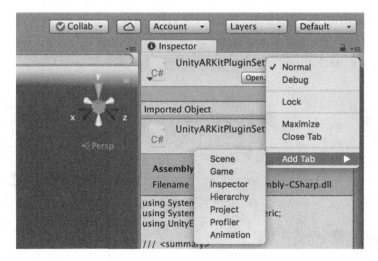

Figure 2-15. *The list of new views*

Floating windows are often covered up by other windows, so the Windows menu on the menu bar has menu items for making each view visible. Notice there is a keyboard shortcut for each, and there is also a Layouts submenu that is identical to the layout menu inside the Editor.

Add and Remove Views

You can also add and remove views in each area using the menu at the top-right corner of the area (Figure 2-15). The Close Tab item removes the currently displayed view. The Add Tab item provides a list of new views for you to choose from.

You may want to have different layouts for different target platforms, or different layouts for development vs. playtesting, or even different layouts for different games. For example, I have a custom layout specifically for my mobile games that pre-saves the Game View in a suitable portrait aspect ratio. It would be a hassle to manually reconfigure the Editor every time you start up Unity. Fortunately, you can name and save layouts by selecting the Save Layout option in the layout menu, which will prompt you for the new layout name (Figure 2-16).

Figure 2-16. *Prompt for new layout*

After saving, the new layout will be listed in the layout menu and also in the list of layouts available for deletion if you select Delete Layout (Figure 2-17).

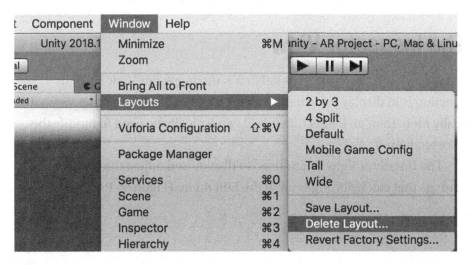

Figure 2-17. *Deletion menu for layouts*

If you've messed up or deleted the original layouts, you can select the Restore Factory Settings option in the area menu (Figure 2-18). This will also delete any custom layouts.

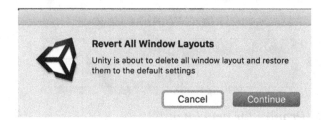

Figure 2-18. *Restore original layout settings*

If you change a layout and haven't saved the changes, you can always discard them by just reselecting that layout in the layout menu.

The Inspector View

The best view to describe in detail first is the Inspector View since its function is to display information about objects selected in other views. It's really more than an inspector since it can typically be used to modify the selected item.

The Inspector View is also used to display and adjust the various settings that can be brought up in the Edit menu (Figure 2-19).

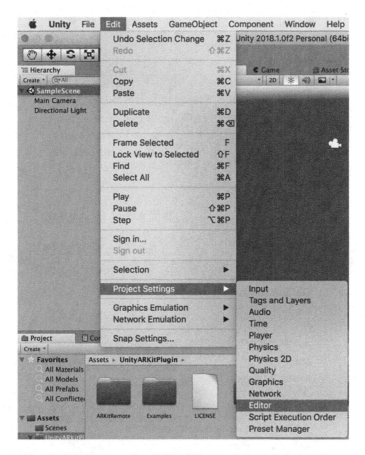

Figure 2-19. *Bringing up the Editor Settings*

The Inspector View displays the Editor Settings. If the project currently has metafiles, then the Version Control Mode is set to Meta Files (and if you're using the Asset Server, this option is set to Asset Server). To hide the metafiles, set the Version Control Mode to Hidden (Figure 2-20).

Figure 2-20. *Editor Settings in the Inspector View*

With the Version Control Mode set to Disabled, Unity will remove the metafiles. The asset tracking is now handled within binary files inside the Library folder of the project.

Note   Unity users who are using metafiles for version control support also have the option of setting Asset Serialization Mode to Force Text. In that mode, Unity scene files are saved in a text-only YAML (YAML Ain't Markup Language) format.

Normally, the Inspector View displays the properties of the most recently selected object (when you bring up the Editor Settings, you really selected it). But sometimes you don't want the Inspector View to change while you're selecting other objects. In that case, you can pin the Inspector View to an object by selecting the Lock option in the menu at the top right of the view (Figure 2-21).

Figure 2-21. *Locking the Inspector View*

The Project View

While the Inspector View can be thought of as the lowest-level View in the Editor, since it displays the properties of just a single object, the Project View can be considered the highest-level view (Figure 2-22). The Project View displays all of the assets available for your game, ranging from individual models, textures, and scripts to the scene files that incorporate those assets. All of the project assets are files residing in the Assets folder of your project (so you might want to think of the Project View as the Assets View).

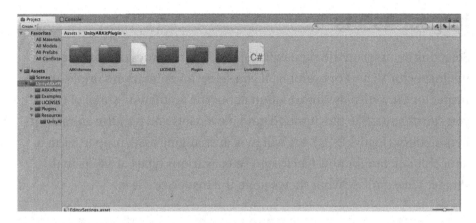

Figure 2-22. *Top level of the Project view*

Switch Between One Column and Two Columns

In several older versions of Unity, the Project View had only a one-column display. That option is still available in the menu for the Project View (click the little three-line icon at the top right of the view), so you can now switch between one and two columns.

Scale Icons

The slider on the bottom scales the view in the right panel—a larger scale is nice for textures, and smaller is better for items like scripts that don't have interesting icons. This is a good reason to partition assets by asset type (i.e., put all textures in a Textures folder, scripts in a Script folder, and so on). Chances are, a single-scale slider setting won't be good for a mixture of asset types.

Inspect Assets

Selecting an asset on the right will display the properties of that asset in the Inspector View. For example, if you select an animation sample, the Inspector View displays information about the animation, some of which you can change, like the duration, and it even lets you play the animation in the Editor (Figure 2-23). We will look at changing asset properties in a later chapter, but for now feel free to select various types of assets in the Project View and see what shows up in the Inspector View.

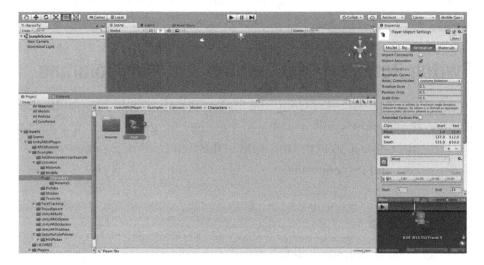

Figure 2-23. *Inspecting a selected asset in the Project View*

Search for Assets

In a large and complex project, it's difficult to manually search for a particular asset. Fortunately, just as in the Finder, there is a search box that can be used to filter the results showing in the right panel of the Project view. In Figure 2-24, the Project View displays the result of searching for assets with "add" in their names.

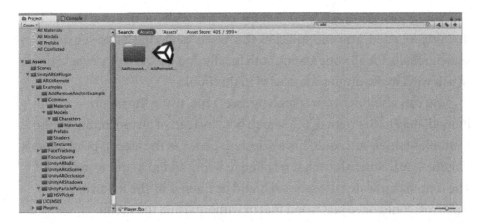

Figure 2-24. *Searching for assets with "add" in the name*

The right panel displays the search results for everything under Assets (i.e., all of our assets). The search can be narrowed further by selecting one of the subfolders in the left panel. For example, if you know you're looking for a scene, and you've arranged your assets into subfolders by the type of asset, you can select the folder to search. In Figure 2-25, I have searched the examples folder for any asset with add in the file name.

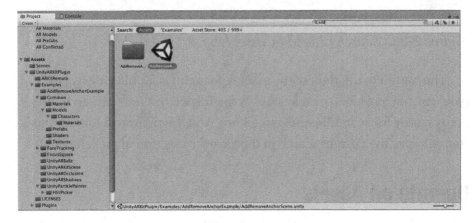

Figure 2-25. *Searching assets in a specific folder*

Notice just below the search; there is a tab with the name of the folder that was selected. You can still click the Assets tab to the left to see the search results for all your assets, both locally and on the Unity Asset Store, which we'll make numerous uses of in this book.

You can also filter your search by asset type, using the menu immediately to the right of the search box. Instead of just searching in the Examples folder, you could have selected scenes as the asset type of interest (Figure 2-26). Notice how that resulted in being added to the search box. The t: prefix indicates the search should be filtered by the following asset type. You could have just typed that in without using the menu.

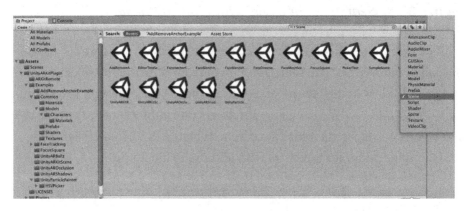

Figure 2-26. *Search filtered by asset type*

The button to the right of the asset type menu is for filtering by label (you can assign a label to each asset in the Inspector View), which is also pretty handy for searching the Asset Store. And the rightmost button, the star, will save the current search in the Favorites section of the left panel.

Operate on Assets

Assets in the Project View can be manipulated very much like their corresponding files in the Finder.

Double-clicking an asset will attempt to open a suitable program to view or edit the asset. This is equivalent to right-clicking the asset and selecting Open. Double-clicking a scene file will open the scene in this Unity Editor window, just as if you had selected Open Scene in the File menu.

You can also rename, duplicate and delete, and drag files in and out of a folder just as you can in the Finder. Some of the operations are available in the Unity Edit menu and in a pop-up menu when you right-click on an asset. You'll get some practice with that in the next few chapters.

Likewise, in the next chapter, you will work on adding assets to a project. That involves importing a file or importing a Unity package, using the Assets menu on the menu bar or just dragging files into the Assets folder of the project using the Finder.

The Hierarchy View

Every game engine has a top-level object called a *game object* or *entity* to represent anything that has a position, potential behavior, and a name to identify it. Unity game objects are instances of the class GameObject.

Note   In general, when we refer to a type of Unity object, we'll use its class name to be precise and make clear how that object would be referenced in a script.

The Hierarchy View is another representation of the current scene. While the Scene View is a 3D representation of the scene that you can work in as you would with a content creation tool, and the Game View shows the scene as it looks when playing the game, the Hierarchy View lists all the GameObjects in the scene in an easily navigable tree structure.

Inspect Game Objects

When you click a GameObject in the Hierarchy View, it becomes the current Editor selection, and its components are displayed in the Editor. Every GameObject has a Transform Component, which specifies its position, rotation, and scale, relative to its parent in the hierarchy (if you're familiar with the math of 3D graphics, the Transform is essentially the transformation matrix of the object). Some components provide a function for the game object (e.g., a light is a GameObject with a Light Component attached). Other components reference assets such as meshes, textures, and scripts. Figure 2-27 shows the components of the Main Camera GameObject (in the Hierarchy view, the entire Player tree of GameObjects is displayed in blue because it's linked to a prefab, a special type of asset that is used to clone a GameObject or group of GameObjects).

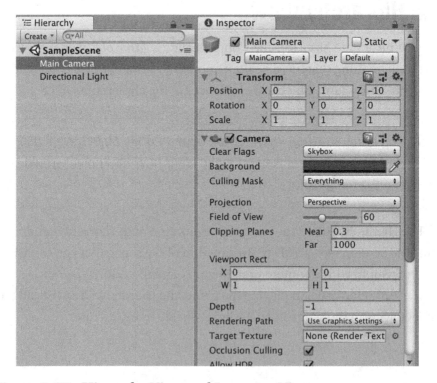

Figure 2-27. Hierarchy View and Inspector View

Parent and Child GameObjects

You will find that many of the GameObjects are arranged in a hierarchy, hence the name of this view. Parenting makes sense for game objects that are conceptually grouped together. For example, when you want to move a car, you want the wheels to automatically move along with the car. So, the wheels should be specified as children of the car, offset from the center of the car. When the wheels turn, they turn relative to the movement of the car. Parenting also allows us to activate or deactivate whole groups of game objects at one time.

The Scene View

Whereas the Hierarchy View allows us to create, inspect, and modify the GameObjects in the current scene, it doesn't give us a way to visualize the scene. That's where the Scene View comes in. The Scene View is similar to the interfaces of 3D modeling applications. It lets you examine and modify the scene from any 3D vantage point and gives you an idea how the final product will look.

Navigate the Scene

If you're not familiar with working in 3D space, it's a straightforward extension from working in 2D. Instead of just working in a space with x and y-axes and (x,y) coordinates, in 3D space, you have an additional z-axis and (x,y,z) coordinates. The x- and z-axes define the ground plane, and y- is pointing up (you can think of y as height).

Note   Some 3D applications and game engines use the z-axis for height and the x and y-axes for the ground plane, so when importing assets, you might have to adjust (rotate) them.

The viewpoint in 3D space is usually called the *camera*. Clicking the x, y, and z arrows of the multicolored Scene Gizmo in the upper-right corner is a quick way of flipping the camera so that it faces along the respective axis. For example, clicking the y arrow gives you a top-down view of the scene (Figure 2-28), and the text under the Scene Gizmo says "Top."

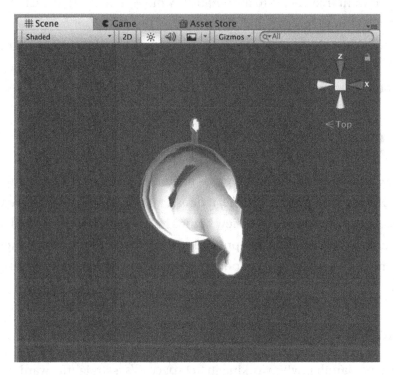

Figure 2-28. *A top view in the Scene View*

The camera here is not the same as the Camera GameObject in the scene that is used during the game, so you don't have to worry about messing up the game while you're looking around in the Scene View.

To demonstrate how to use the Navigation tools, I have selected the Player GameObject from the Project Folder and dragged this to the Hierarchy View.

Clicking the box in the center of the Scene Gizmo toggles the camera projection between perspective, which renders objects smaller as they recede in the distance; and orthographic, which renders everything at their original size whether they are close or far. Perspective is more realistic, and what you normally use in games, but orthographic is often more convenient when designing (hence its ubiquity in computer-aided design applications). The little graphic preceding the text under the Scene Gizmo indicates the current projection.

You can zoom in and out using the mouse scroll wheel or by selecting the Hand tool in the upper-right toolbar of the Editor window and click-dragging the mouse while holding the Control key down. When the Hand tool is selected, you can also move the camera by click-dragging the view, and you can rotate (orbit) the camera by dragging the mouse while holding the Option (or Alt) key down, so you're not restricted to just the axis camera angles, like in Figure 2-29.

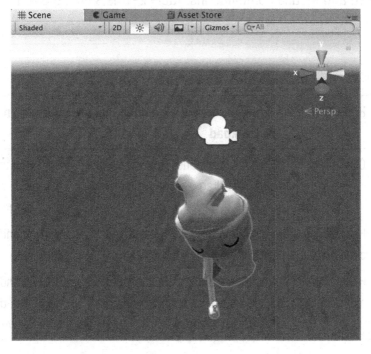

Figure 2-29. *A tilted perspective in the Scene View*

Notice that when you're looking from an arbitrary angle, the text under the Scene Gizmo says Persp or Iso, depending on whether you're using perspective or orthographic projection (Iso is short for isometric, which is the tilted orthographic view common in games like StarCraft).

The other buttons on the toolbar activate modes for moving, rotating, and scaling GameObjects. There's no reason to change them at the moment, so those modes will be explained in more detail when you start creating new projects.

Tip   If you accidentally make a change to the scene, you can select Undo from the Edit menu. If you made a lot of changes you don't want to keep, you could just decline to save this scene when you switch to another scene or exit Unity. In the meantime, note that you can still move the camera while in those modes, using alternate keyboard and mouse combinations. Table 2-1 lists all the possible options.

Table 2-1. *Available Scene View Camera Controls*

Action	Hand tool	1-button mouse or trackpad	2-button mouse	3-button mouse
Move	Click-drag	Hold Alt-Command and click-drag	Hold Alt-Control and click-drag	Hold Alt and middle click-drag
Orbit	Hold Alt and click-drag	Hold Alt and click-drag	Hold Alt and click-drag	Hold Alt and click-drag
Zoom	Hold Control and click-drag	Hold Control and click-drag or two-finger swipe	Hold Alt and right-click drag	Hold Alt and right-click drag or scroll wheel

There are a couple of other handy keyboard-based scene navigation features. Pressing the Arrow keys will move the camera forward, back, left, and right along the x–z plane (the ground plane). And holding the right mouse button down allows navigation of the scene as in a first-person game. The AWSD keys move left, forward, right, and back, respectively, and moving the mouse controls where the camera (viewpoint) looks.

When you want to look at a particular GameObject in the Scene View, sometimes the quickest way to do that is to select the GameObject in the Hierarchy view, then use the Frame Selected menu item in the Edit menu (note the handy shortcut key F). In Figure 2-28, I clicked on the x-axis of the Scene Gizmo to get a horizontal view, then selected the Player GameObject in the Hierarchy View, and pressed the F key (shortcut for Frame Selected in the Edit menu) to zoom in on and center the player in the Scene View.

You can also select a GameObject directly in the Scene View, but you have to exit the Hand tool first. Just as selecting a GameObject in the Hierarchy View will result in that selection displaying in the Scene View and Inspector View, selecting a GameObject in the Scene View will likewise display that selection in the Inspector View and display it as the selected GameObject back in the Hierarchy view. In Figure 2-30, after I invoke Frame Selected on the Player, I clicked the Move tool (the button directly right of the Hand tool button in the top right corner of the Editor window) and then clicked a GameObject near the Player in the Scene View. The Hierarchy View automatically updates to show that GameObject is selected, and the GameObject is also displayed in the Inspector View.

Figure 2-30. *Selecting a GameObject in the Scene View*

Scene View Options

The buttons lining the top of the Scene View provide display options to assist in your game development. Each button configures a view mode.

The leftmost button sets the Draw mode. Normally, this mode is set to Textured, but if you want to see all the polygons, you can set it to Wireframe (Figure 2-31).

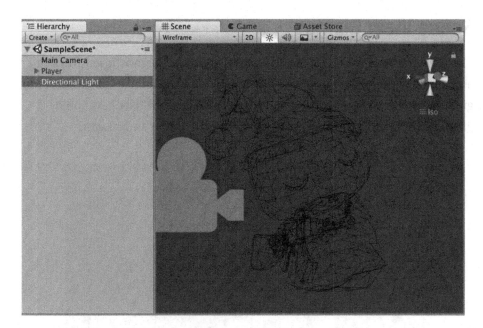

Figure 2-31. *Wireframe display in the Scene view*

The next button sets the Render Paths, which controls whether the scene is colored normally or for diagnostics.

The three buttons to the right of the Render Paths mode button are simple toggle buttons. They each pop up some mouse-over documentation (otherwise known as *tooltips*) when you let the mouse hover over them.

The first of those controls the Scene Lighting mode. This toggles between using a default lighting scheme in the Scene View or the actual lights you've placed in the game.

The middle button toggles the Game Overlay mode, whether the sky, lens flare, and fog effects are visible.

And finally, there is the Audition Mode, which toggles sound on and off.

Scene View Gizmos

The Gizmos button on the right activates displays of diagnostic graphics associated with the Components. The Scene View in Figure 2-32 shows some gizmos. By clicking the Gizmos button and checking the list of available gizmos, you can see those icons representing a Camera and a Light.

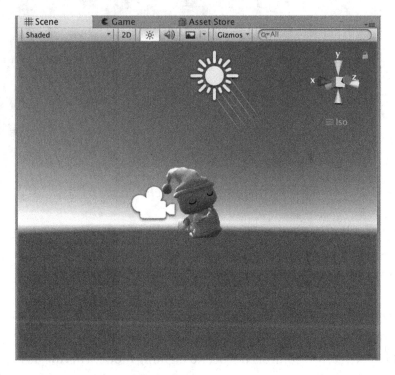

Figure 2-32. *Gizmos in the Scene View*

You can select and deselect the various check boxes in the Gizmos window to focus on the objects you're interested in. The check box at the top left toggles between a 3D display of the gizmos or just 2D icons. The adjacent slider controls the scale of the gizmos (so a quick way to hide all gizmos is to drag the scale slider all the way to the left).

The Game View

Now let's look at the Game View. Like the Hierarchy View and Scene View, the Game View depicts the current scene, but not for editing purposes. Instead, the Game View is intended for playing and debugging the game.

The Game View appears automatically when you click the Play button at the top of the Unity Editor window. If there isn't an existing Game View when you click Play, a new one is created. If the Game view is visible while the Editor is not in Play mode, it shows the game in its initial state (i.e., from the vantage of the initial Camera position).

The Game View shows how the game will look and function when you actually deploy it, but there may be discrepancies from how it will look and behave on the final build target. One possible difference is the size and aspect ratio of the Game View. This can be changed using the menu at the top left of the view. Figure 2-33 shows what happens when you switch from the Free Aspect ratio, which adjusts to the dimensions of the view, to a 5:4 aspect ratio, which results in the scaling down the game display so that it fits within the area and maintains the chosen aspect ratio.

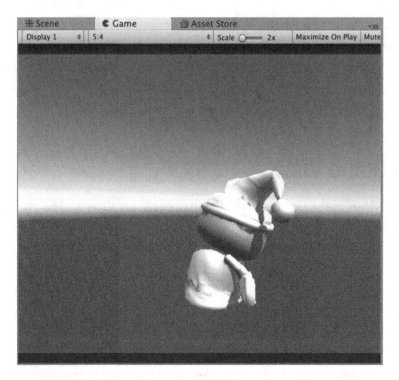

Figure 2-33. *The Game view*

Maximize on Play

Clicking the Maximize on Play button will result in the Game view expanding to fill the entire Editor window when it is in the Play mode (Figure 2-34). If the view is detached from the Editor window, the button has no effect.

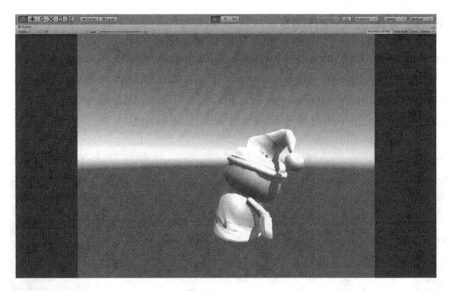

Figure 2-34. *Game view with Maximize on Play*

Stats

The Stats button displays statistics about the scene (Figure 2-35) that update as the game runs.

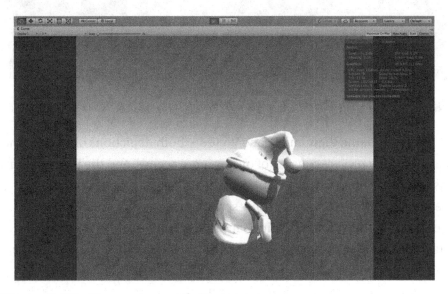

Figure 2-35. *Game view with Stats*

Game View Gizmos

The Gizmos button activates displays of diagnostic graphics associated with the Components. The Game View in Figure 2-36 shows two icons that are gizmos for an Audio Source. The list to the right of the Gizmos button allows you to select which gizmos you want displayed.

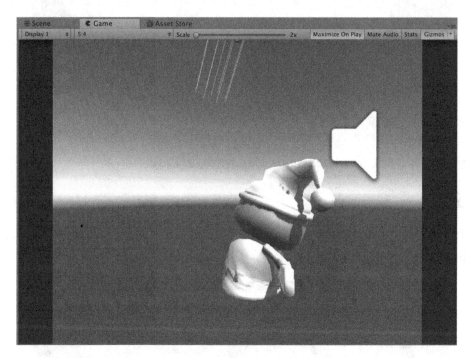

Figure 2-36. Game View with Gizmos

Both the Game View and Scene View are both depictions of the current scene. A Unity project consists of one or more scenes, and the Unity Editor has one scene open at a time. Think of the project as a game and the scenes as levels (in fact, some Unity script functions that operate on scenes use "level" in their names). Unity GameObjects are made interesting by attaching Components, each of which provides some specific information or behavior. That's where the Inspector View comes in. If you select a game object in the Hierarchy View or Scene View, the Inspector View will display its attached components.

The Console View

The remaining view in all the preset layouts, the Console View, is easy to ignore but it's pretty useful (Figure 2-37).

Figure 2-37. *The Console view*

Informational, warning, and error messages appear in the Console View. Errors are in red, warnings in yellow, and informational messages in white. Selecting a message from the list displays it with more detail in the lower area. Also, the single-line area at the bottom of the Unity Editor displays the most recent Console message, so you can always see that a message has been logged even if the Console view is not visible.

Tip   Warning messages are easy to ignore, but you can ignore them at your risk. They are there for a reason and usually indicate something has to be resolved. And if you let warnings accumulate, it's difficult to notice when a really important warning shows up.

The Console can get cluttered pretty quickly. You can manage that clutter with the leftmost three buttons on top of the Console View. The Clear toggle button removes all the messages. The Collapse toggle button combines similar messages. The Clear on Play toggle will remove all messages each time the Editor enters Play mode.

The Error Pause button will cause the Editor to halt on an error message, specifically when a script calls a Log.LogError.

While operating in the Editor, log messages end up in the Editor log, while messages generated from a Unity-built executable are directed to the Player log. Selecting Open Player Log or Open Editor Log from the view menu (click the little icon at the top right of the Console View) will bring up those logs, either in a text file or in the Console app (Figure 2-38).

Figure 2-38. *The Unity logs in the Mac Console app*

Explore Further

We've come to the end of this Unity tour. In Chapter 3, you'll start learning some of the ARKit features. This is the first chapter that really starts using Unity. You haven't yet started building your own scene (that will begin in Chapter 3), but you've been able to get familiar with the Unity Editor. There are plenty of official Unity resources that expand on the topics I will be covering.

Unity Manual

As you can see, there's a lot of Unity user interface, and we've hardly covered it all. This is a good time to get serious about reading the Unity Manual, either from within the Unity Editor (the Welcome screen or the Help menu) or on the Unity website (`http://unity3d.com/`) under the Learn tab in the "Documentation" section. The web version is pretty handy when you want to look something up or just read about Unity without having a Unity Editor running nearby.

Most of what was covered in this chapter match topics in the Unity Basics section of the Unity Manual, particular the sections on "Learning the Interface," "Customizing Your Workspace," "Publishing Builds," and "Unity Hotkeys." We did jump ahead into the Advanced section of the Unity Manual and touch on Unity's support for version control. That's covered more in-depth with the Unity Manual's page on "Using External Version Control with Unity."

Tutorials

Besides the "Documentation" section, the Learn tab on the Unity website also includes a "Tutorials" section that features an extensive set of Beginning Editor videos. As the name implies, these videos introduce the Unity Editor, and in fact the set of videos covers much of what was discussed in this chapter, including descriptions of the most important views (the Game View, Scene View, Hierarchy View, Inspector View, and Project View) and even the process of publishing a build.

Version Control

Although I only discussed version control briefly, in the context of explaining how to remove metafiles, that topic is worth a little more discussion, since a version control system (or VCS) is so important to software development (which you'll realize the first time you lose your project or can't remember what change you made that broke your game!). If you already have a favorite VCS, you may want to use it with Unity, and if you haven't been using one, then you may want to consider it if only to keep old versions of your project around in case you need to roll back, with the ability to check differences between versions,

Among version control systems, Perforce is a popular commercial tool used in game studios, and Subversion (svn) has a long history as an open source option. These days, distributed version control systems like Git and Mercurial are trending. I use Mercurial on Bitbucket (`http://bitbucket.com/`) for my internal projects and post public projects on GitHub, including the projects for this book.

To say Unity VCS support is product agnostic is really another way of saying Unity doesn't have any particular version control system integrated into the Unity Editor. The metafiles, and YAML scene files for Unity Pro users, simply provide better compatibility with text-oriented version control systems that are commonly used for source code. You still have to run the VCS operations yourself outside of Unity. You can find out more about YAML, by the way, on `http://yaml.org/`.

I find it convenient to use the Mac GitHub app provided on the GitHub website and similarly SourceTree for BitBucket, also available on that website.

CHAPTER 3

The Unity ARKit

Now that you have installed Unity and the Unity ARKit Plug-in, it's time to get to learn a bit more about this tool and make our first AR experience. Note, I called this an experience and not a game, although it could possibly be used as a game in some way; from my point of view a game needs some key elements, which I will go into detail in Chapter 4.

If you have not already opened the AR Project we created in the last chapter, now would be a good time to do this. If you look in the Project folder (Figure 3-1) and look in each folder, you will see that the Unity ARKit Plug-in comes with a number of resources that we will explore and use throughout this book.

Creating a Scene

The first task we are going to do is create GameObject and put it in our scene and look at it in AR. From the Menu, select GameObject ➤ 3D Object ➤ Cube (Figure 3-1). We could choose any of the 3D objects, but I want you to see the Cube in AR and move around it in 3D space. Although I prefer Spheres, the 3D Cube has six vertices (the angular point of a polygon), and these are going to be easier to see. We will, however, add different shaped game objects very soon.

© Allan Fowler 2019
A. Fowler, *Beginning iOS AR Game Development*,
https://doi.org/10.1007/978-1-4842-3618-5_3

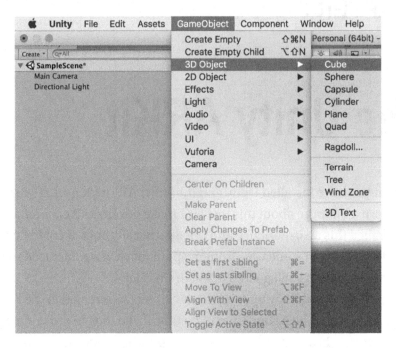

Figure 3-1. *Creating a 3D GameObject*

Once you have completed this task, you will see our amazing Cube in the Scene panel (Figure 3-2).

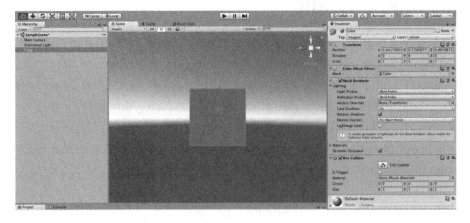

Figure 3-2. *The Cube GameObject in the Scene*

Now let's have a look in the Inspector (Figure 3-3). If your Transform positions are not the same as mine, don't worry about this for now (we are going to move the GameObject anyway). Note the scale is 1,1,1. Unity uses the metric standard for measurement, and therefore 1 unit in Unity space is the equivalent of 1 meter in real-world terms. Now for most traditional games (that are not AR), this is not really something that beginner developers need to worry about (much). However, because we will be projecting the game assets into a real-world space, getting measurements and scale correctly become very important. So, if we leave the scale of our Cube at 1 meter wide, by 1 meter tall, by 1 meter deep, this is going to be a pretty big cube. The convention for describing coordinates in 3D graphics is X,Y,Z. I will use this standard throughout this book. I am going to scale our amazing Cube, so it is going to fit into my very small apartment. It might surprise a few readers that most authors of instructional books don't live in multi-million-dollar mansions (well at least this author doesn't).

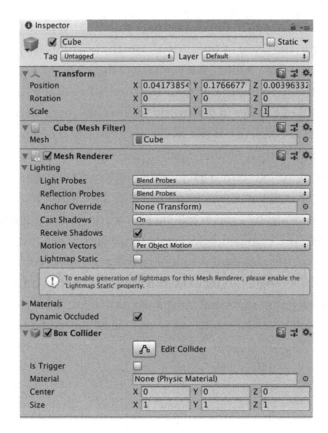

Figure 3-3. *The Cube GameObject in the Inspector*

In the Inspector, set the scale to 0.25,0.25,0.25 (Figure 3-4).

Figure 3-4. *The Cube GameObject reduced Scale*

Now if you look at the Cube in the Scene, it will (or should) look smaller (Figure 3-5). If you want to want a closer look at the GameObject, you can move the camera in the Scene view closer to the Cube. There are two main ways of moving the Scene view camera. The easiest way is by selecting the GameObject in the Hierarchy panel and pressing the f key (I remember this as f for focus). The other way is to use the middle mouse wheel (if you have a 3-button mouse) to move the camera in or out or double tab the mouse (if you have a Magic Mouse). I'm (very) old school and prefer to use my 5-button mouse.

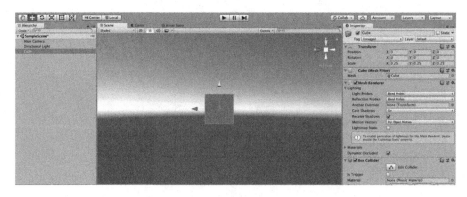

Figure 3-5. *The Scene view of the Cube GameObject at reduced Scale*

Cameras

Now would be a good time to talk about cameras. We just moved the camera in the Scene view. This camera enables you, the developer, to see what is in the Scene. However, if you look in the Hierarchy panel, you will see a GameObject Main Camera. This is the camera that the player will be looking through. You will note in Figure 3-5, there is a camera icon in my Scene view. This is where the Player's camera is positioned in the scene.

I want you to select the Main Camera in the Hierarchy panel. You will see a small window in the lower right of the Scene view a small window (Figure 3-6). This window displays a view from the Player's camera (Camera Preview).

Figure 3-6. *Camera Preview*

Although the Camera Preview window provides us with a good idea of what the scene will look like to the player, to get a better view, we can select the Game view tab (Figure 3-7).

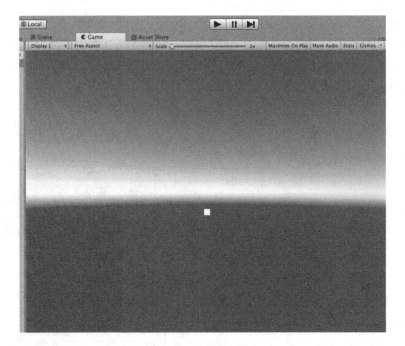

Figure 3-7. *The Game view*

As we saw in the previous chapter, there are a number of settings that we can use (aspect ratio, scale, and so on). We can see here that our amazing Cube is a bit far away. We are going to first move the Game Object, and then we are going to move the Main Camera.

Transformation

There are several ways to move (transform) a GameObject in Unity. The first way we will use (and is the main method I use) is to set the transform settings in the Inspector. First, select the GameObject we want to transform. Then, in the inspector set the transform positions to 0,0,0 (Figure 3-8).

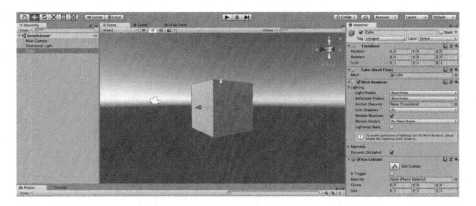

Figure 3-8. *The GameObject with the updated Transform positions*

Now let's have a look in the Main Camera to check what this looks will like to the player (Figure 3-9).

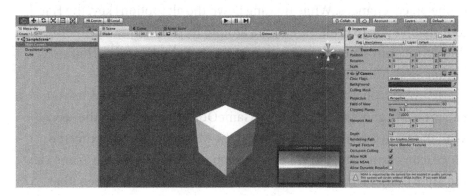

Figure 3-9. *Camera Preview of the GameObject with reset Transform positions*

You will note that the GameObject is still a bit too far away from the Main Camera. At the top left of the screen (just above the Hierarchy panel), there are six icons (Figure 3-10).

Figure 3-10. *Six transform icons*

The first icon is the Hand tool (Q shortcut), and it is used for transforming (or panning) the camera in the scene view. With this tool selected, select any GameObject in Hierarchy move mouse and note that the transform settings of the GameObject don't change, but the view of the GameObject changes. While holding down the alt (option) key, the Hand tool enables you to orbit the camera around its pivot point. By holding down the control button, you can move (or dolly) the camera closer or farther away from the GameObject.

The next icon is the Move tool (W shortcut). The move tool, as you can probably guess, is for moving a GameObject's position in the scene. With the Main Camera selected, select the Move tool (by selecting the Move icon or pressing the W key), and you will note that in the Scene view the Main Camera icon now has the move Gizmo (the Red, Green Blue lines with arrow points – Figure 3-11). First, select the Green line (Y-axis) and move the Main Camera down. Note that when you select this line, the other arrow lines are grayed out and the line you selected changes to yellow. Now try to move the camera to 0 on the Y-axis. You will note that this might take some time. You might want to enter zero in the Y in the Inspector if you can't get the placement correct (which is why I prefer to type the values in the Inspector).

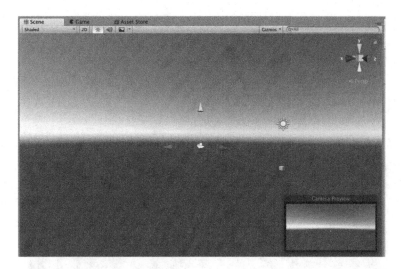

Figure 3-11. *The move Gizmo*

The next tool is the Rotate tool (E shortcut). As you probably guessed, this tool is used for rotating the GameObject. Try selecting the Cube and then press the R key. You will see the Rotate Gizmo (Figure 3-12). With the Rotate Gizmo, you can change the rotation of the GameObject by clicking and dragging the axes of the wireframe Rotate Gizmo that appears around it. With the Rotate Gizmo, the red, green, and blue circles perform a rotation around the red, green, and blue axes (red is the x-axis, green is the y-axis, and blue is the z-axis). The outer circle is used to rotate the GameObject around the Scene view z-axis.

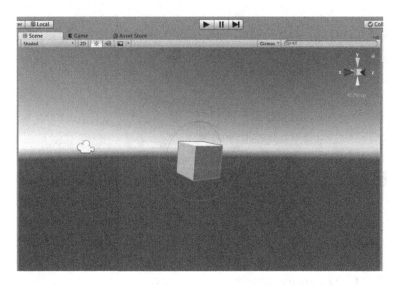

Figure 3-12. *The rotate Gizmo*

The next tool is the Scale toll (R shortcut). The scale tool is used to scale or rescale GameObjects on all axes by selecting the center of the Scale Gizmo and then dragging the mouse (Figure 3-13). You can also use this tool to scale on an individual axis by selecting any one of the individual axes.

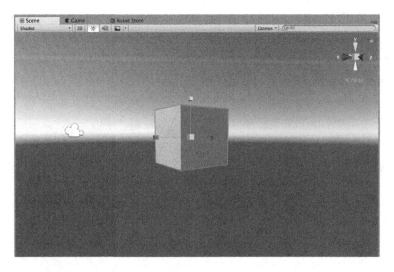

Figure 3-13. *The scale Gizmo*

Scaling the Cube with the Cube GameObject selected sets the position of the cube, or it has been moved while we were using the transform tools; now would be a good time to set or reset the position to 0,0,0 (Figure 3-14).

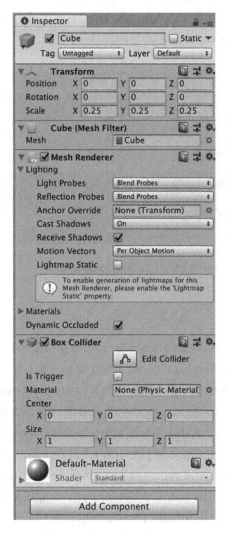

Figure 3-14. *The Cube GameObject Position settings*

Now we need to position the Main Camera at the origin (0,0,0). If you look at the position of my cube, this would mean our camera will be right in the middle of our Cube. So, let's first move the cube out of the way. Set the Cube transformation position settings to 0,0,1 and then move the Main Camera to 0,0,0 (Figure 3-15). Now the cube will look like it is positioned 1 meter away from our camera.

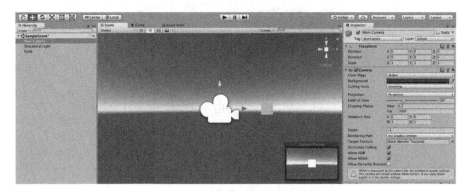

Figure 3-15. *The new Main Camera settings*

Testing

Now it's time to see how our amazing cube is going to look in the real world. When developing for iOS, we need to use Xcode before we can test or deploy the game. To publish an AR game on iTunes, we need to submit the game to Apple for approval, and then when it gets approved, we can download it from the iTunes store and see what it looks like on our device. With Xcode, we can preview what our game will look like on our device, but this still requires us to build and run the game and use Xcode to preview the game. As you might imagine, this was a very time-consuming (and a little bit frustrating) experience. Unity came to the rescue and provided us with Unity Remote. Unity Remote is an application (or app) available for iOS devices in the iTunes app store. This tool helps us test a game on an iOS device without the need for submitting the game to the iTunes store. However, at the time of writing, Unity Remote (version 5) does not support AR. The fine people at Unity have thought about this challenge and have included in the Unity ARKit a small program called UnityARKitRemote. Unity ARKitRemote provides us with the tools needed to test our AR project on an iOS device.

ARKit Remote

In the Project folder, type in a search text to find the ARKit Remote Prefab (Figure 3-16). Now drag this file to the Hierarchy tab (Figure 3-17).

Figure 3-16. *Searching for the ARKit Remote*

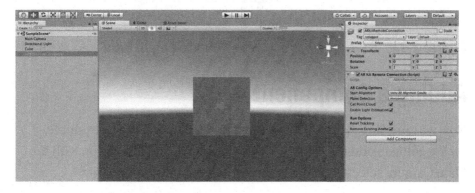

Figure 3-17. *The ARKitRemote Prefab in the Hierarchy*

Setting Up the Main Camera

Now in the Main Camera settings, set the clear flags to Depth only (Figure 3-18).

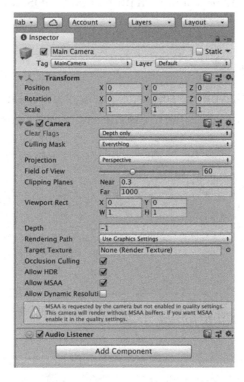

Figure 3-18. *Set the Camera's Clear Flags to Depth only*

Adding a Component

Now we are going to add a Component to our camera. In this example, we are going to add the Unity AR Video script. To add this script, with the Main Camera selected, in the Inspector select Add Component.

In the Inspector, you will see a list of possible components that you can add (Figure 3-18). It might take you a while to find it, so I recommend using the search bar in the Add Component menu for the Script we are looking for. In Figure 3-19, in the search bar, I searched for video.

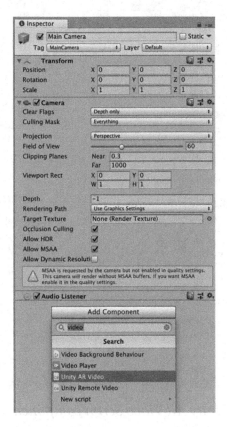

Figure 3-19. *Searching for the Unity AR Video Script component*

Once you have found the Unity AR Video script, select it (single mouse-click) and now you should see this component is now added to the Main Camera (Figure 3-20).

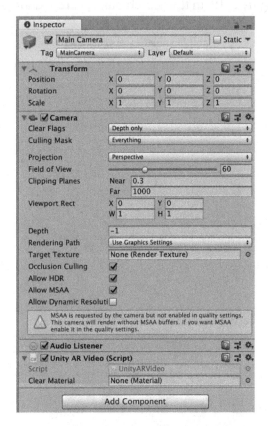

Figure 3-20. *The Unity AR Video Script component added to the main camera*

In the Unity AR Video script, there is a property called Clear Material. We are going to add a material. In the Unity AR Video script Clear Materials properties, on the right of the properties box, there is a small gear (Figure 3-19); if you select this gear, you will see a list of all the possible materials available in this project folder (Figure 3-21). Again, you can search for this manually, or use the search bar. Search for the YUV material. I will go into a bit more detail on what this material is doing and why we use it in a later chapter.

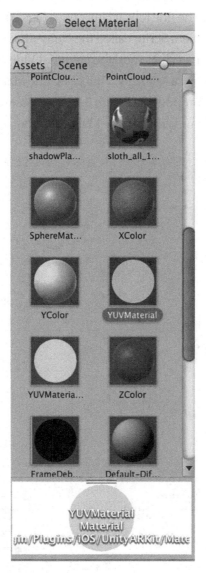

Figure 3-21. *Selecting the YUV material for the Clear Material*

Tracking the Phone Movement

To make the AR project look real, we need to track the movement of the phone in the real world and project an accurate representation of the virtual object on the phone's screen. The fine folk at Unity have (again) made our lives easier and in the Unity ARKit has a Script called the Unity AR Camera Manager. Following the steps that we did to add the Unity AR Video script, we are going to add the Unity AR Camera Manager. First select the Main Camera and in the Inspector, select Add Component (Figure 3-22); now search for AR Camera Manager (Figure 3-23), and add it to the Main Camera.

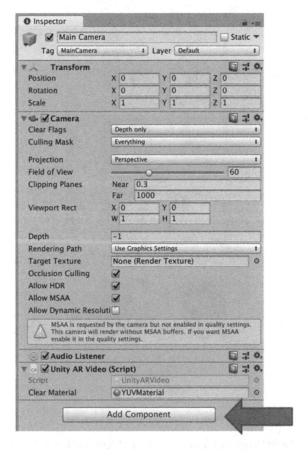

Figure 3-22. *Add Component*

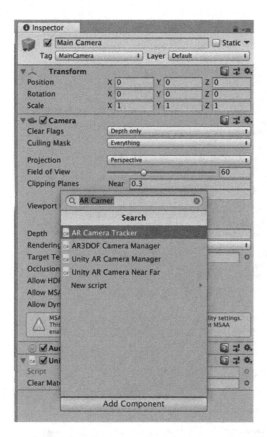

Figure 3-23. *Searching for the Unity AR Camera Manager*

It is good practice to add the Main Camera to the Tracked Camera
Properties of the Unity AR Camera Manager; this will ensure that the AR
Camera Manager uses the correct camera. However, if you don't select
this, the Unity AR Camera Manager will choose it for you. To add the Main
Camera to the Camera Properties of the Unity AR Camera Manager, select
the Main Camera from the Hierarchy and drag this to the Tracked Camera
properties of the Unity AR Camera Manager (Figure 3-24).

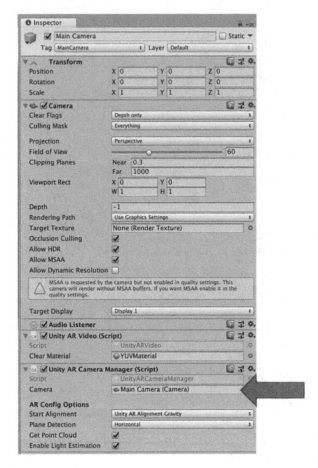

Figure 3-24. Setting the Main Camera as the Tracked Camera

Build and Run

Now we are ready to build and run our app. Make sure you have connected your iOS device to your Mac and then select Build & Run from the Unity File menu (Figure 3-25). If you have not already downloaded the latest version of Xcode, you need to do this now (it's going to take a while).

Figure 3-25. *Selecting Build & Run*

Figure 3-26. *The Build Settings*

In the Build setting menu, first select the Platform you want to build this on, which in our example will be iOS. Also, select the Development Build check box. Finally, it is really important to select only the scene you want to build. If your current scene is not listed, click the Add Open scenes button (Figure 3-26) and uncheck any other scene.

From the Build Setting screen, select the Player Settings icon. This will open the Inspector for the Player Settings where we will enter the Company Name and Product Name (Figure 3-27).

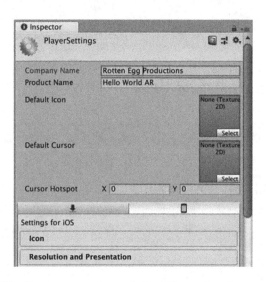

Figure 3-27. *The Inspector view of the PlayerSettings*

Scroll down the menu to find the Bundle Identifier (Figure 3-26). It is important to note that once you have registered a bundle identifier to a Personal Team in Xcode, the same bundle identifier cannot be registered to another Apple Developer Program team in the future. This means that when you are testing your game using a free Apple ID and a Personal Team, you should choose a bundle identifier that is for testing only - you won't be able to use the same bundle identifier to release the game. The best solution to do this is to add "Test" to the end of the test bundle identifier - for example, com.yourCompanyName.yourAppNameTest. Also note that the bundle identifier is written in what is known as reverse-DNS style. The accepted characters are alphanumeric characters, periods, and hyphens. In my example (Figure 3-28), I have used com. RottenEggProductions.HelloWorldARTest as the bundle identifier (You will need your own name). If you have a signing team ID, you may want to include that as well. But for testing purposes, this is not needed.

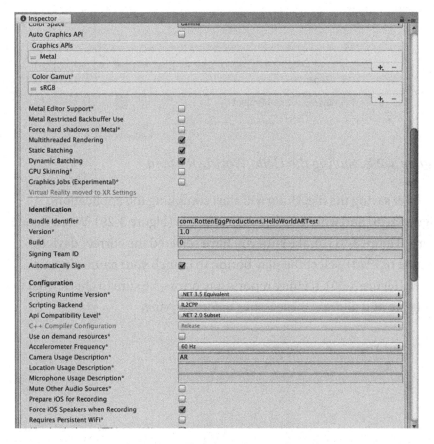

Figure 3-28. Setting the Bundle Identifier in the PlayerSettings

Now select the Build and Run icon. Unity will Prompt you to Save the Project. The tradition when learning Introductory Programming courses is to name our first application Hello World (don't ask me why). So, in this tradition, I am going to name my first AR App, Hello WorldAR. Note in Figure 3-29, I am saving this in the same folder as my Unity Project. Some people would argue that this is not good practice, but it's good enough for now.

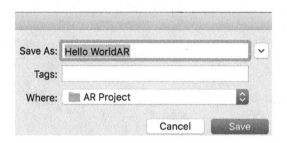

Figure 3-29. *Saving the Hello WorldAR Menu*

After saving the file, Unity will start compiling the application (Figure 3-28) and will eventually open Xcode (Figure 3-29). When Xcode opens (Figure 3-31), make sure you have selected the correct device (iPhone or iPad), select the play button to launch your game on your device (Figure 3-30). If Unity reports any errors, be sure to check what the errors are and address these issues before retrying.

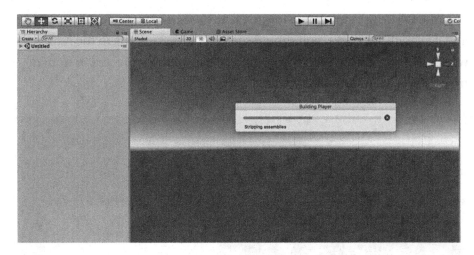

Figure 3-30. *Unity Compiling our application*

Figure 3-31. *Xcode*

You will be prompted to allow the Unity ARKit to access your camera and if everything works, you should see your amazing cube in the real world. In my example, you can see my amazing cube projected in front of my photo of Mount Aoraki (Figure 3-32).

Figure 3-32. *My Hello WorldAR app*

Saving the Scene

Now would be a good time to save our scene. From the file menu, select File ➤ Save Scene As and name this scene (Figure 3-33). I have chosen Hello WorldAR as the name of this Scene (Figure 3-34).

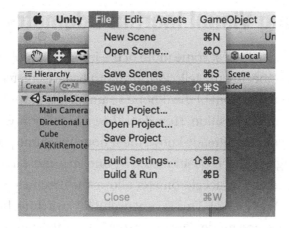

Figure 3-33. *Save Scene as menu*

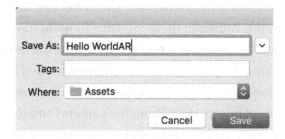

Figure 3-34. *Saving the Scene and selecting its location*

Understanding Scenes

Now might be a good time to discuss the difference between Unity scenes and projects. A Unity Project contains all the scenes and necessary code that might be used for the game or application. A Scene is an element (or component) of the project. Think of the project as an entire movie and the scenes as parts of that movie. In a game, those scenes could be the menus, levels, credits, and so on.

Introducing Visual Inertial Odometry

Now we are going to look at some more of the important tools used for creating an AR game. In our Hello WorldAR project, we created a cube that was positioned in front of the iPhone's camera and stayed there while we moved the camera position. How does the camera know where it is positioned? As you may already know, the iPhone has some pretty cool ways of knowing where it is positioned. The one I use most frequently is the accelerometer. The accelerometer allows the iPhone to know its position in 3 Axes (X,Y,Z). This is very useful for switching between portrait and landscape mode. The other tool I use is the compass (or magnetometer), and as you probably already know, this is very useful for navigation. The last tool is the gyroscope. The gyroscope tracks the rotation or twist of the iPhone. Although these are great tools for navigation, they do not have the level of precision needed for tracking the movement of the phone in AR. To track the movement of the iPhone needed for AR, Apple recently included some technologies in the phone's camera. Through combining the Visual information (from the camera) and the Inertial information (from the accelerometer and the gyroscope), it is possible to accurately measure the position of the iPhone.

Feature Points

So how does the camera track the position of the phone? Good question! The camera in the iPhone (currently iPhone 8 or higher) is smart enough to identify key points (or feature points) in the real world and when the camera is moved, track where these points are. This process requires some pretty impressive mathematics, but the more recent iPhones have enough processing power to do this.

Point Clouds

The Unity ARKit includes a prefab for helping the phone identify feature points in the physical world. The first one we are going to use is the PointCloud Prefab.

With your Hello WorldAR app open in Unity, we are going to create an empty GameObject. From the file menu, select GameObject ➤ Create Empty (Figure 3-35).

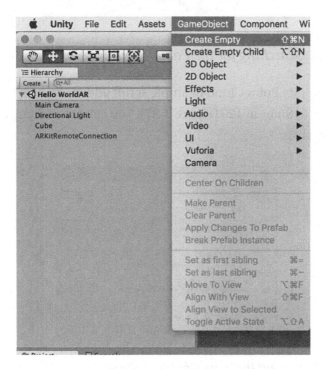

Figure 3-35. *Creating an empty GameObject*

With the Empty GameObject Selected in the Inspector, rename it Point Cloud. Now add a component. In the search bar, search for the Unity Point Cloud Example and add this to the Point Cloud GameObject (Figure 3-36).

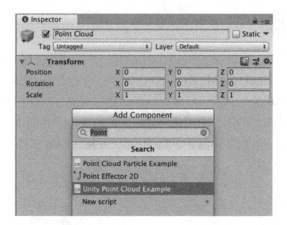

Figure 3-36. *Searching for the Point Cloud Example*

With the Unity Point Cloud Example script added, now set the number of Max Points to Show at 120 (Figure 3-37). You can set as many Point Clouds as you like.

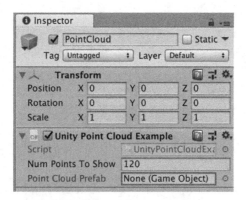

Figure 3-37. *Setting the Max Points to Show*

Now we need to add a Point Cloud Particle Prefab to Point Cloud. Select the small gear to the right of the Point Cloud Prefab box and then search for Prefab (Figure 3-38). Select and drag the PointCloudPrefab to the Point Cloud Particle Prefab box in the Point Cloud Particle Example script (Figure 3-39).

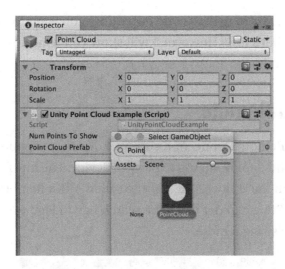

Figure 3-38. *Searching for the PointCloud Prefab*

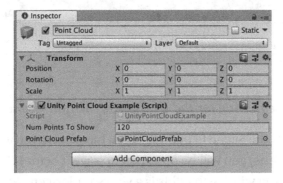

Figure 3-39. *The PointCloudPrefab set as the Point Cloud Prefab*

Testing

Now we are going to test our Point Cloud. When we tested our Hello WorldAR app, we went through the long (and possibly tedious) task of building the App, launching it in Xcode. and then finally being able to see our App on our iOS device. The wonderful people at Unity have thought about this and have created a way for us to reduce the time of testing our development. In the Unity ARKit, there is a Scene that will enable us to preview the build in the Game tab of Unity. If you want to go through the process of using Xcode every time you want to preview the development, that's fine. However, I will show you a more efficient way that you might value.

Unity ARKitRemote

Because Unity Remote Connection currently does not support AR, we need to build and deploy an App to our iOS device. The fine folk at Unity have included in the Unity ARKit, a scene called ARKit Remote. You can find this in the Project folder using the search bar. In Figure 3-40, I have used the search string remote.

Figure 3-40. *Searching for the UnityARKitRemote Scene*

Double-click the Scene to open it. If you have not saved any changes to the current scene, you will be prompted to save it before Unity will open another scene. You will see that this is a very simple Scene that consists of a Main Camera and a Directional Light (Figure 3-41).

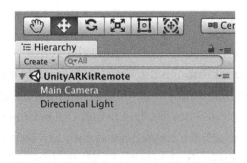

Figure 3-41. *UnityARKitRemote*

If you select the Main Camera in the Hierarchy, you will see that the Main Camera has several scripts added (Figure 3-42). These scripts will enable the phone camera to track its position as well as enable us to see the camera view in the Unity Editor.

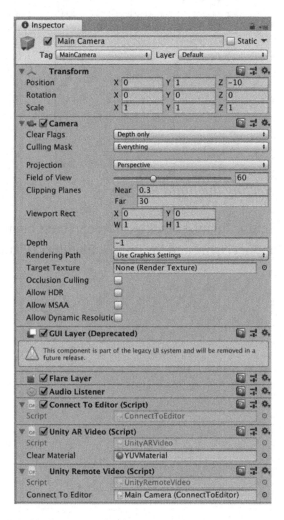

Figure 3-42. *Main Camera Scripts*

Just like we did with the Hello WorldAR app that we created, we need to deploy this App to our phone. From the file menu, select File ➤ Build Settings (Figure 3-43).

Figure 3-43. *Selecting the Build Settings*

In the Build Setting menu, select the Player Settings menu and make changes to the Product Name and the Bundle Identifier (Figure 3-44).

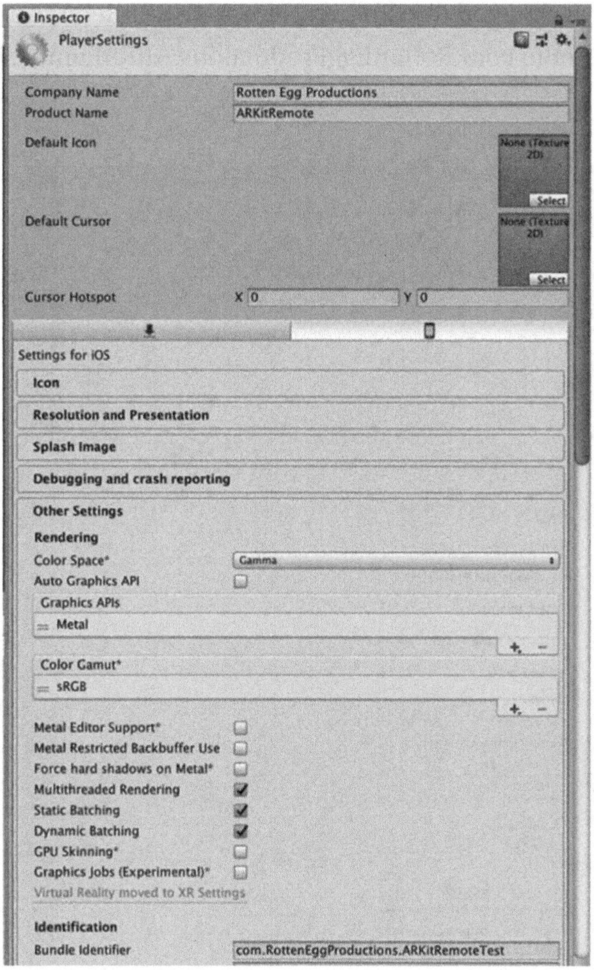

Figure 3-44. The Inspector view of the PlayerSettings

Note, I have changed the Product Name to ARKitRemote and the
Bundle Identifier to com.RottenEggProductions.ARKitRemoteTest
(Figure 3-45).

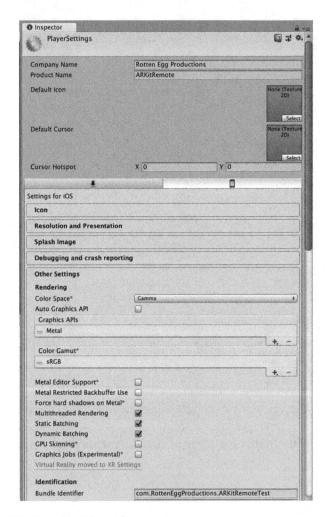

Figure 3-45. *Bundle Identifier settings*

Make sure you have the correct Scene to build and select Build and Run from the Build Menu. Now Unity will compile our App and run Xcode and Xcode will deploy this to our Device (Figure 3-46).

Figure 3-46. *ARKitRemote installed on my iPhone*

Now we need to add the ARKit Connection Prefab to our Hello WorldAR project. Open your Hello WorldAR Scene (double-click).

Using ARKit Remote Connection

In the Project Folder, search for a Prefab called ARKitRemoteConnection (Figure 3-47).

Figure 3-47. *Searching for the UnityARKitRemoteConnection Prefab*

Select this Prefab and add it to the Scene (drag it to the Hierarchy) (Figure 3-48).

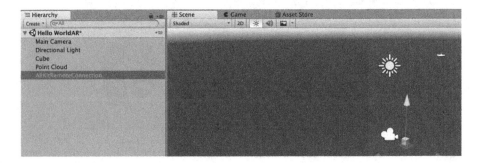

Figure 3-48. *The UnityARKitRemoteConnection in the Scene*

Now we are going to open the ARKitRemote on our iOS device. In Unity, open up the Hello World AR scene and then select the Game tab and press the Play button. Unity will prompt you to connect to player in the console menu (Figure 3-49).

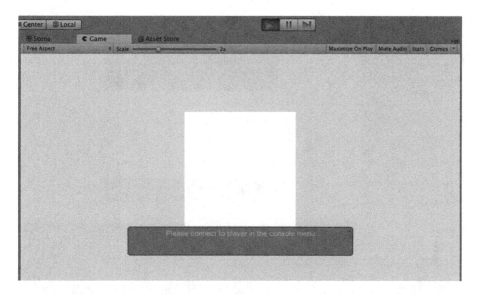

Figure 3-49. *Unity connect to player message*

In the Console table, select Editor and select your iOS device (Figure 3-50).

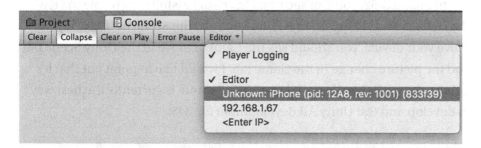

Figure 3-50. *Selecting the iOS device in the Console menu*

Then Unity will prompt you to Start Remote ARKit Session (Figure 3-51). Click the icon on the Game screen in Unity and your application can now run on your iOS device.

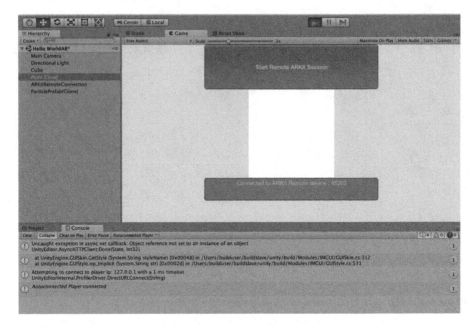

Figure 3-51. *Start Remote ARKit Session prompt*

In Figure 3-52, you can see that I have successfully been able to view the Hello WorldAR app on my iPhone and see the Scene in Unity. If you move your device, you should see the Camera move in the Unity Scene tab and the picture change in the Game tab. I would like to point out that it's going to be a bit slow (lag), but the ARKitRemote is currently the best way to develop and test Unity AR development for iOS.

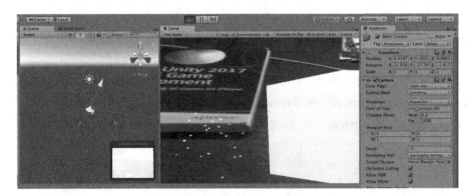

Figure 3-52. *The Cube and the Point Cloud in the Game View*

While the point cloud system is great for identifying a non-symmetric object (like a sofa). It will be more efficient and more effective if we use another feature provided in the UnityARKit that will help identify a flat plane (like a floor, wall, or table).

Plane Visualization

First, create another empty GameObject that will contain the scripts needed. To create an Empty GameObject, from the menu, select GameObject ➤ Create Empty (Figure 3-53).

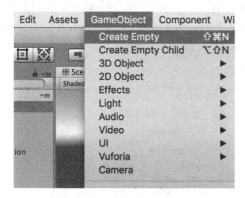

Figure 3-53. *Creating an Empty GameObject*

With the GameObject selected, in the Inspector, name this Created Planes (Figure 3-54).

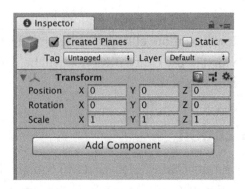

Figure 3-54. *Naming the new GameObject Created Planes*

Now we need to add a component. Select the Add Component button in the Created Planes Inspector and in the search bar, search for the Unity AR Generate Plane script (Figure 3-55).

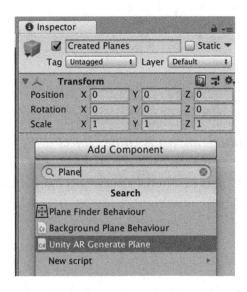

Figure 3-55. *Searching for the Unity AR Generate Plane script*

With the Unity AR Generated Plane script included in the Created Planes GameObject, in the Plane Prefab setting of the Unity AR Generated Plane script. select the small gear to the right of the option box and search for and select the DebugPlanePrefab (Figure 3-56).

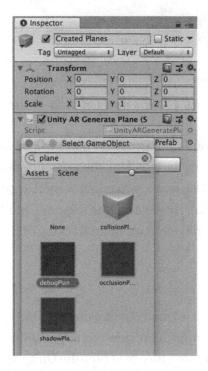

Figure 3-56. *Searching for the debugPlanePrefab*

Testing

Now with your iOS device connected to your Mac, run the UnityARKitRemote App. Now in Unity. connect to your device in the Editor and click the Play button. With your iOS device, turn the camera to view a flat surface, and you should see your point cloud and a rectangle in the Unity Game view screen (Figure 3-57).

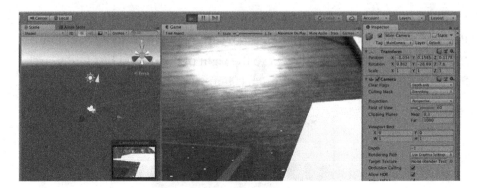

Figure 3-57. *The Point Clouds and Created Plane*

Both the Point Clouds and Created Planes will be useful in the game that we create for finding and tracking the reference points from the iOS camera. If you are feeling brave, you might want to try deploying the final build to your iOS device. However, at the moment, our Cube is not quite ready for really using the reference point tracking of the camera.

Summary

In this chapter, we have learned about using the Unity ARKit and configuring our iOS device to preview our applications and games in real time. We also learned some theory of how the Unity ARKit can track the position of the device. Finally, we used some tools to help us accurately track the fine movements of the device.

CHAPTER 4

Hit Testing and Lighting

In our last chapter, we used both Cloud Points and Generated Planes to help the camera track the movement of the device. However, you may have noticed that our amazing cube continued to stay at the point of origin. While this may be okay for our first AR App, I'm sure in time you might want to create virtual objects that appear to be located on a physical object in the real world. To do this, we are going to use a feature of the Unity ARKit called hit testing. You may have also noted that the lighting of the GameObject on the screen of your iOS device is not consistent with the lighting in the real world; we are also going to address this issue in this chapter.

Hit Testing

Hit testing will enable us to place something on the Generated Planes we created in Chapter 3. This will also enable the AR App to place an object to look like it is in a position in the real world that is relative to where the user taps on the screen of their device.

Let's open the Hello WorldAR scene we created in the last chapter. With the Hello World AR Scene open in Unity, now select the Created Planes GameObject in the Hierarchy (Figure 4-1).

© Allan Fowler 2019
A. Fowler, *Beginning iOS AR Game Development*,
https://doi.org/10.1007/978-1-4842-3618-5_4

Figure 4-1. *Selecting the Created Planes GameObject in the Hierarchy*

With the Created Planes GameObject selected in the Hierarchy, select Add Component; and in the search bar, search for the Editor Hit test (Figure 4-2). Now select this to add it to our Created Planes Game Object. This script will enable us to test out the basic functionality of Hit Testing in the editor.

Figure 4-2. *Searching for the Editor Hit Test*

By now you might be keen to include something in the AR App a bit more interesting than our cube. We could search the Asset Store for an interesting or relevant asset to include, or we could create our own one. As making our own game assets is very time consuming and outside of the scope of this book, for now, let's use one of the existing assets in the Unity ARKit. In the Project folder search for the asset Player (Figure 4-3). If this GameObject is not included in the version of the Unity ARKit you download, it can be downloaded from the Unity Asset Store (`https://assetstore.unity.com/packages/essentials/tutorial-projects/survival-shooter-tutorial-40756`).

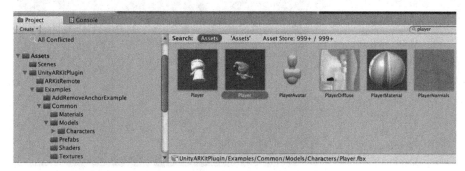

Figure 4-3. *Searching for the Player game asset*

With this asset selected, drag it to the Hierarchy (Figure 4-4).

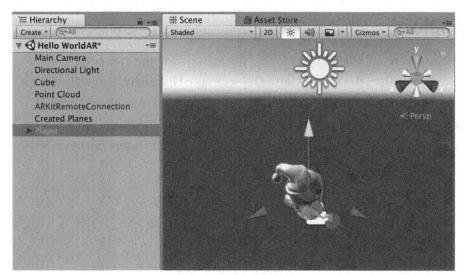

Figure 4-4. *The Player character added to the Hierarchy*

Now it's time to say goodbye to our amazing cube. Select the Cube in the Hierarchy and right-click and select delete (Figure 4-5).

Figure 4-5. *Deleting the Cube*

Scale

You might recall that in Chapter 2, I discussed the importance of scale in AR. If you select the Player GameObject in the Hierarchy, you will see that this asset is 1 meter tall. Now, this may be fine, but I want to make this asset look a lot smaller in the real world. I suspect that this is the intention of the person that created this asset. With the Player GameObject selected, change the scale to .25,.25,.25 (Figure 4-6).

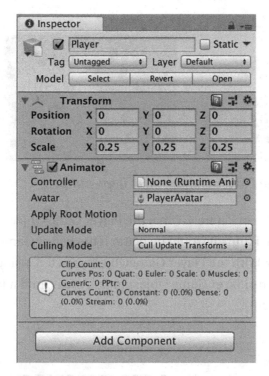

Figure 4-6. *The Rescaled Player GameObject*

Transformation

If you select the Main Camera and look at the Camera Preview window, you will notice that our Player GameObject is not visible to the player. If you look at the Inspector or both the Main Camera and the Player GameObjects, you will see that the positions of both of these assets are 0,0,0. Let's move the Player GameObject. With the Player, GameObject selected, in the Inspector change the position to 0,0,1 (Figure 4-7).

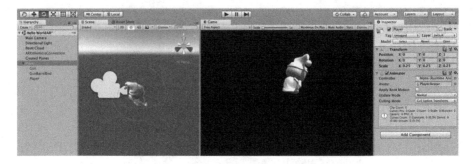

Figure 4-7. *The Player GameObject Repositioned*

You will notice in Figure 4-7 that the Player GameObject is facing away from the camera. I think it would be better if the Player GameObject was facing the player. With the Player GameObject selected, using the rotate tool, and rotate the Player Game Object in the Y-axis until it faces the main Camera (Figure 4-8).

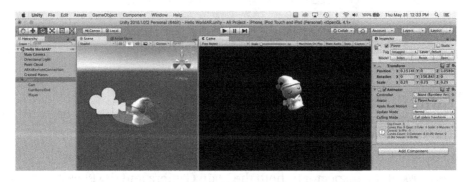

Figure 4-8. *Rotating the Player GameObject*

When rotating a GameObject, it is possible to also unintentionally change another axis. In Figure 4-8, notice how the Transform positions of the X-axis and the Y-axis have also changed. Let's reset the positions of the X-axis to 0 and the Z-axis to 1. I prefer whole numbers, so I am going to set the rotation of the Y-axis to 156 (Figure 4-9).

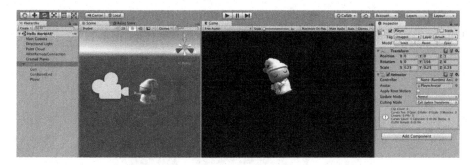

Figure 4-9. *The rotated Player GameObject*

The Editor Hit Test Script

Now select the Editor Hit Test script that is in the Created Planes GameObject. The Editor Hit Test script has three changeable parameters: the Hit Transform, the Max Ray Distance, and the Collision Layer Mask (Figure 4-10).

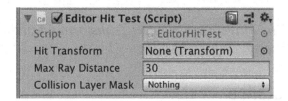

Figure 4-10. *Editor Hit Test script*

Hit Transform

The Hit Transform parameter box specifies the transform of the GameObject. In our example, this will be the x,y,z of our Player GameObject that will be moved to where the player has selected. The Editor Hit test script does not currently support tap or touch, so in this case, the GameObject will be positioned where the player clicked in the Game tab of the Unity Editor.

Select the Player GameObject in the Hierarchy and drag this to the Hit Transform property box in the Hit Editor Test script (Figure 4-11).

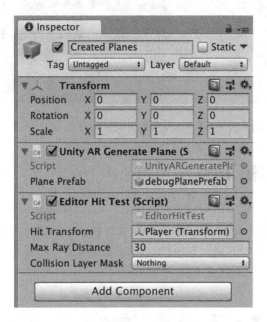

Figure 4-11. *The Player GameObject Transform set in the Hit Transform property*

Max Ray Distance

For this exercise, we are not going to change the Max Ray Distance. If you are interested in learning about this parameter, there is a wealth of information on Ray Casting on the Internet. In summary, it is the process of casting an invisible ray to detect if anything (like a collider) is in the path of the ray.

Collison Layer mask

The Collision Layer Mask drop-down menu has several options (Figure 4-12).

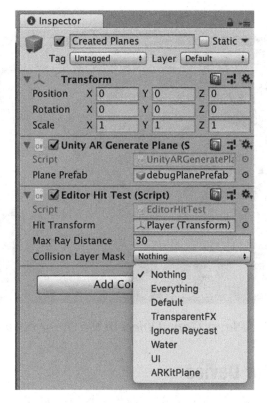

Figure 4-12. *The Collision Layer Mask options*

We are going to select the ARKitPlane option. The Collision Layer Mask option sets what collision layer mask to take into consideration during hit testing. In our case, we will select the ARKitPlane.

Testing

Now connect your iOS device to your Mac and run the UnityARKitRemote App on your device. In the Console in Unity, select your device from the Editor, and press the Play button. In the Game Screen, click the Start ARKitRemote icon, and then move the device slowly for the camera to find suitable planes. When you see a plan in the Game tab of Unity, click inside that plane, and you will see your Player avatar in the Game view screen (Figure 4-13).

111

Figure 4-13. *The Player GameObject in the Game view screen*

Testing On Our Device

Now that we have successfully been able to test our AR App in the editor, it's time to see what it looks like on our device. You may recall during our test build, we added the Editor Hit Testing script. This script is very useful for testing our App in the editor, but as we found, it does not support tap or touch user interaction on our device. If we want to test the App on our device, there is a better option.

Removing a Component

To remove the Editor Hit Testing script component from the Created Plane GameObject, we need to select the Gear on the right (Figure 4-14). Select the Remove Component option.

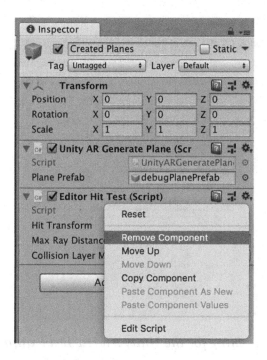

Figure 4-14. *Remove Component menu option*

Adding a Component

Now let's add a component that will support a fully functional user interaction on our device. In the Inspector of our Created Planes GameObject, select the Add Component button and in the search bar search for hit (Figure 4-15). Now select the Unity AR Hit Test Example Script to add it to our Created Plane GameObject (4-16).

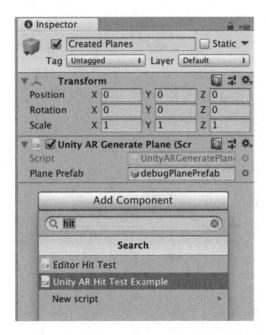

Figure 4-15. Searching for the Unity AR Hit Test Example

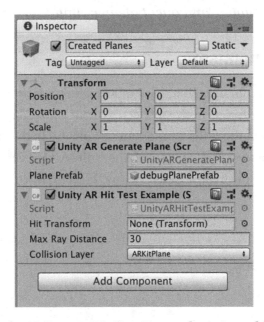

Figure 4-16. The Unity AR Hit Test Example script added to the Generated Planes GameObject

Adding the Hit Transform

As we did with the Editor Hit Test Example, we need to add the Hit Transform parameters. To do this, select the Player GameObject and drag it to the Hit Transform properties box in the Unity AR Kit Test Example (Figure 4-17). If the ArKitPlane is not set as the Collision Layer, using the drop-down menu, change this to ARKitPlane.

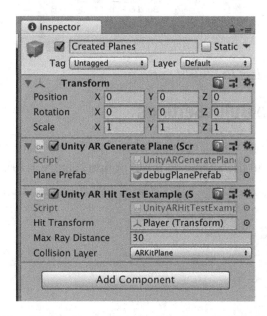

Figure 4-17. *The Player Transform added to the Hit Transform properties*

Preparing to Deploy

Before we build and run our new App, we need to change the Build settings. From the menu, select File ➤ Build Settings (Figure 4-18).

Figure 4-18. Select the Build Settings

Changing the Build Settings

In the Build Settings menu, check that you are building the current scene (Hello WorldAR) in the Scenes to Build option (Figure 4-19).

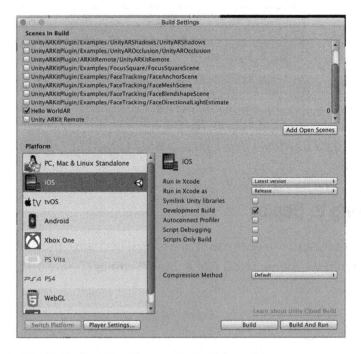

Figure 4-19. Selecting the Scenes to Build option

116

Select the Player Settings and in the Inspector, change the Product Name and Bundle Identifier (Figure 4-20).

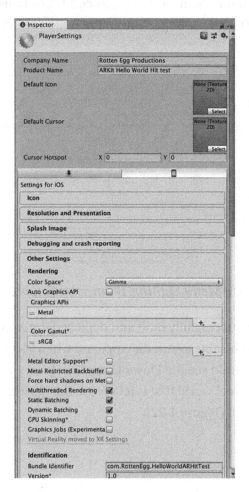

Figure 4-20. *PlayerSettings Inspector*

Before we select Build and Run, I recommend opening Xcode first and making sure we have selected the target device and have set the Team in Signing menu (Figure 4-21). If you don't select this now, you will encounter a build failed message. Now in the Build Settings menu. select the Build and Run.

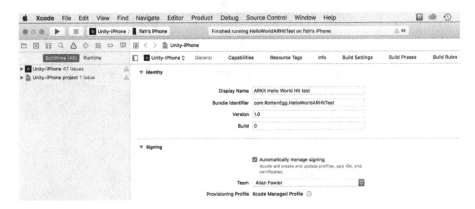

Figure 4-21. *Xcode Menu Signing Team selection box*

After you have successfully built and deployed the App to your iOS device, you should be able to run the App; and when you tap the screen on your device, you should see the Player GameObject on your screen placed in a position in the real world that is relative to the position of where you tapped on the screen (Figure 4-22).

Figure 4-22. *The Hello WorldAR App deployed on an iPhone*

While our Player GameObject is a lot more interesting than our cube, we can improve this App. If we look at the lighting of the Player GameObject, the lighting is not completely consistent with the lighting in the real world. We are going to change the lighting of the AR image, so it is closer to the lighting in the real world. My children think we should rename our Player GameObject to Nightmare Chaser, so let's also rename our Player GameObject to Nightmare Chaser.

Changing the Player GameObject Name

Changing the Player GameObject name can be done by selecting this GameObject in the Hierarchy and then in the Inspector, select the current name and typing in our new name (Figure 4-23). Another option is to Right-Click the Player GameObject in the Hierarchy and select the Rename option from the drop-down menu (Figure 4-24).

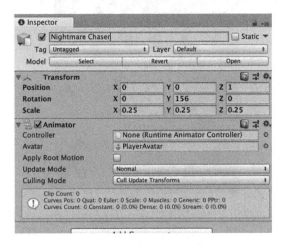

Figure 4-23. *Changing the Player GameObject's name in the Inspector*

Figure 4-24. *Changing the Player GameObject's name in the Hierarchy*

Lighting

Some of you might have noticed that the lighting of the Nightmare Chaser was not consistent with the lighting in the real world. Once again, the fine people at Unity have provided us with a solution (for the record, I have no affiliation with Unity; I do think they did a great job on the Unity ARKit).

Turning Off the Lights

We are going to use a different light source for our App. However, for best results, let's make sure we have turned off all the lights in the scene.

From the Main Menu, select Window ➤ Lighting ➤ Settings (Figure 4-25).

***Figure 4-25.** Selecting the Lighting Settings*

In the Lighting Settings, in the Environment settings change the Intensity Multiplier to zero. In the Mixed Lighting settings, uncheck the Baked Illumination settings (Figure 4-26).

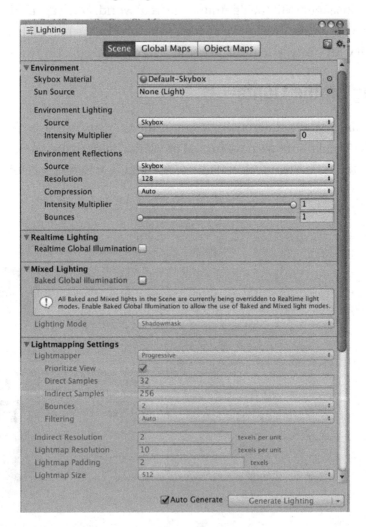

Figure 4-26. *Changing the Lighting Settings*

Now select the Directional Light and in the Inspector, change the color to white. There are a number of ways to change the color. First in the Inspector, select the color properties box and a color selector will appear

(Figure 4-27). In the Color selector menu, there is a color selector wheel to select the color. To use this wheel, select and drag the small color selection circle until you find a color that is close to what you want. In the center of the circle, there is a square for selecting the tone. Once you have selected a color close to the one you want, then you can use the small circle in the square to refine your choice. This method may work for some people, but I just type in the RGB or HSV values of the color that I want in the properties box (Figure 4-28).

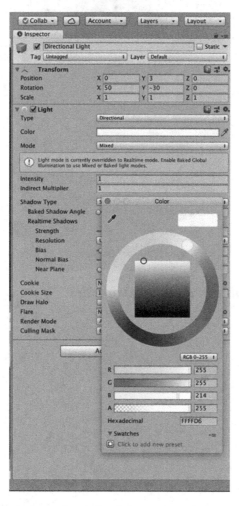

Figure 4-27. *Using the color wheel*

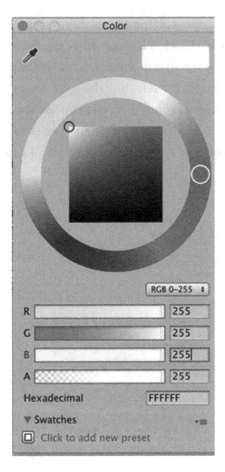

Figure 4-28. *Typing in the color properties*

Setting the Ambient Light Source

Now we can set the ambient light source. With the Directional Light selected, select the Add Component button and search for ambient (Figure 4-29).

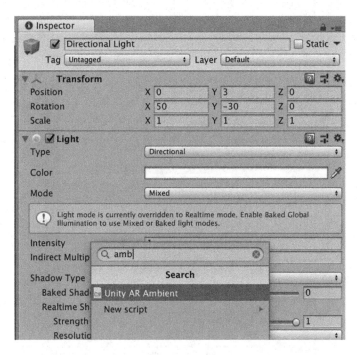

Figure 4-29. *Searching for the Unity AR Ambient Component*

You will see that the Unity ARKit has also included a script called Unity AR Ambient. Select this script to add it to our directional light (Figure 4-30).

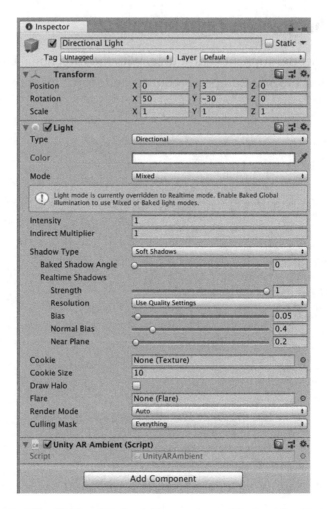

Figure 4-30. *The Unity AR Ambient script added to the Directional Light*

This script estimates the real-world lighting and will make changes to the lighting in our App. This will make our App look more realistic. Now let's test this app under different lighting conditions. By now, you should already know how to build and run the scene. Before we do this, I would recommend making one small change in the Player Settings.

Build and Run – Version Control

I am a huge fan of version control. I think it is good practice to save our work with a different version number when making any major or minor change. In fact, when writing this book, I have used version control. I have had too many instances of my system crashing and not being able to recover the last version of a project I was working on. Thankfully, most times, I have a prior version that I can use and get back to work relatively quickly.

Because we already have a prior version of our Hello WorldAR Hit test, I am going to save this next test with a different version number. Select Build Settings from the main menu and then select Player Settings (Figure 4-31). In the Inspector of the Player settings, scroll down to see the Identification settings, and under the Version change the version to 2.0. Some people might argue that the version should be 1.1 (as this is only a minor change), but as long as we change the version number, that is what is most important.

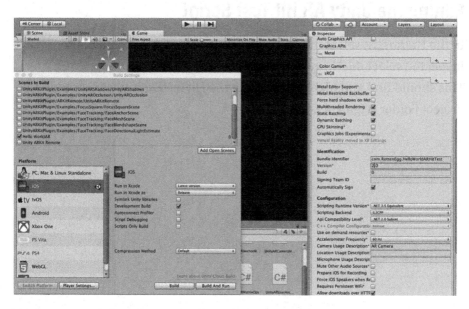

Figure 4-31. *The Changing the Version Identification in the Inpsector view*

127

Now open Xcode, make sure you are signed in, and connect your iOS device to your Mac and select Build and Run. If your build is successful, you should notice the lighting in the App changing under different lighting conditions.

Positioning the Camera

You may have discovered that even though we carefully positioned our Nightmare Chaser so that he faced the player camera, he does not always face the camera when we run the App on our device. The position of the Nightmare Chaser will depend on where your iOS device is facing when you start the App. Although this is a book for beginners, we are going to have to write some code. Hopefully, this will not be too painful for you. This code is going to automatically rotate our Nightmare Chaser to face the camera every time we start the App.

Editing the Unity AR Hit Test Script

In the Hierarchy, select the Created Planes GameObject; and in the Inspector. select the UnityARHitTestExample in the Script Properties box. This should find and highlight the UnityARHitTestExample.cs script in the Project Folder (Figure 4-32).

Figure 4-32. *Selecting the UnityARHitTestExample.cs script*

If you do not have a copy of Visual Studio or Mono Develop, I highly recommend downloading a copy and installing this now. Although we won't be writing a lot of code throughout this book, if you are serious about developing AR games for iOS, then you will need an IDE.

With the UnityARHitTestExample.cs script selected, double-click this file, and it should open in your IDE (Visual Studio or MonoDevelop). On Line 18, enter the following code:

```
//Automatically Face the Camera
m_HitTransform.LookAt (Camera.main.transform.position);
m_HitTransform.eulerAngles = new Vector3 (0, m_HitTransform.
eulerAngles.y, 0);
```

Now save the script and test it to see if this runs. The // adds a comment to the code and is ignored when compiled. If you encounter any runtime errors or bugs with the code, simply comment out these three lines, and it should run (although, our Nightmare Chaser will not automatically be positioned so that it faces the camera).

Summary

In this chapter, we have learned about Hit Testing, which helps our App identify surfaces in the real world and "place" the GameObjects on those surfaces. We also learned how to change the lighting so that it is consistent with the lighting in the real world.

CHAPTER 5

Making AR Games

Now that you have learned some fundamentals of using the ARKit and have a grasp of Unity, we are going to start making an AR Game. Along the way, we will also cover some of the more advanced functions of the ARKit.

Fugu BowlAR Game

Now it's time to create an AR Game. I have decided to resurrect the game that we created in our last book, *Learn Unity for iOS Game Development* (Apress, 2017). In case you are one of the few people that didn't get this book, our game was Fugu Bowl, which was a small bowling game for iOS devices. In our last book, we used JavaScript, but for the AR version, we are going to use C#. Although JavaScript is a great programming language, if you are going to continue to use Unity, then learning C# will be much more important and valuable. If you don't know how to program in C#, I would highly recommend learning this language. The focus of this book is on learning to make an AR Game, so I won't focus on teaching how to program in C#. However, I have included comments in the code to try to help anyone who is not familiar with C# understand what the code is going to do.

© Allan Fowler 2019
A. Fowler, *Beginning iOS AR Game Development*,
https://doi.org/10.1007/978-1-4842-3618-5_5

Creating a New Scene

As we have already downloaded and installed the Unity ARKit package into our AR Project, let's continue to use this. Typically, I prefer (and recommend) starting a new Project for each new game that is created. However, as this would involve downloading the Unity ARKit package, let's pass on doing that this time.

To create a New Scene, from the main menu, select File ➤ New Scene (Figure 5-1). It is probably more efficient to use the shortcut keys (⌘-N), and I will also be including the shortcut keys for frequent commands for those readers who prefer to use them.

Figure 5-1. *Creating a New Scene*

Let's Save our Scene. Select from the main menu, File ➤ Save Scene as (Figure 5-2).

Figure 5-2. *Save Scene as*

You will be presented with the Save As Dialog box (Figure 5-3) and type in the name for our Scene. I have decided to name this game Fugu BowlAR (see what I did there?).

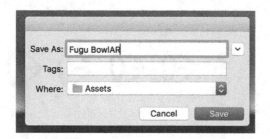

Figure 5-3. *Saving the Scene As Fugu BowlAR*

Select Save to save this Scene. You will note that this file is now saved in the Assets folder. I believe that in software development, it is better to be well organized (some might call this obsessive). Therefore, this Scene should probably be saved in the Scene folder. In the project folder, select the Fugu BowlAR scene (Figure 5-4) and drag it to the Scenes folder (Figure 5-5).

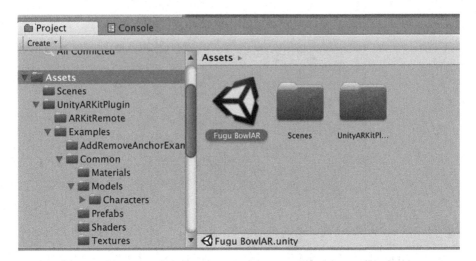

Figure 5-4. *Selecting the Fugu BowlAR Scene in the Project Assets folder*

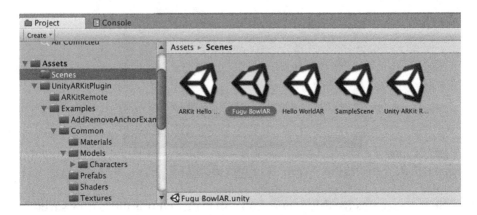

Figure 5-5. *Fugu BowlAR in the Scenes Project folder*

Creating AR Assets

You may recall creating our amazing cube, and we are going to repeat this process. First, we are going to create an amazing bowling ball. We could probably find a really amazing one online or possibly in the Unity Asset

Store, but I'm a big fan of creating my own game assets when I have time and don't have the budget for paying someone with more artistic talent than I do to do this for me (I have very limited artistic talent).

In the main menu, select GameObject ➤ 3D Object ➤ Sphere (Figure 5-6).

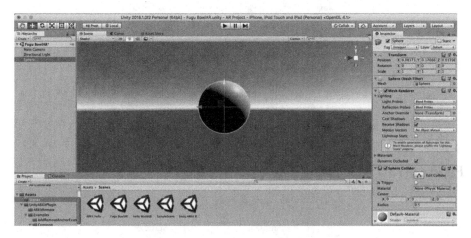

Figure 5-6. *The Sphere GameObject in the Scene*

Let's change some of the properties. The first task is to rename this GameObject. I'm going to name this GameObject BowlingBall. With the Sphere GameObject selected, in the Inspector, select GameObject name (Figure 5-7) and select the current text and type in our new name (Figure 5-8).

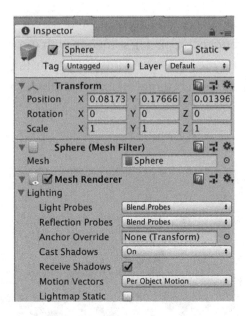

Figure 5-7. *The selected Sphere GameObject*

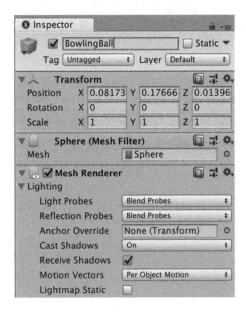

Figure 5-8. *The Sphere GameObject renamed as BowlingBall*

Transform the BowlingBall

You may recall that in Unity we work in metric. This means that our BowlingBall GameObject is going to be 1 meter, by 1 meter, by 1 meter. I haven't spent a lot of time bowling, but even I know that this is going to be a really big bowling ball. Let's resize (scale) it and put the BowlingBall at the origin (0,0,0).

First, select the Scale and type in the following Scale settings 0.25,0.25,0.25. Now let's set the Transform Position to 0,0,0 (Figure 5-9).

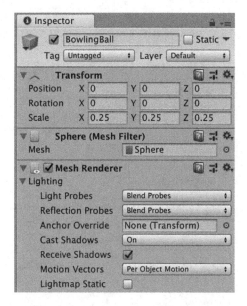

Figure 5-9. *Repositioned and rescaled BowlingBall*

Adding a Rigidbody

When we created our cube, it floated in the air, which was pretty cool. But as we want the ball to roll on a floor in the real world, we need to add a Rigidbody component. The Rigidbody component provides a rigid body simulation that simulates how nonchanging shapes react to forces and collisions. We want our BowlingBall GameObject to react to gravity (stay on the floor, and we are also going to apply some force to it to make it move).

137

Finally, we want it to collide with our bowling pins. So, we need to add a Rigidbody component to our BowlingBall.

With the BowlingBall selected in the Hierarchy view, in the Inspector, select Add Component (Figure 5-10).

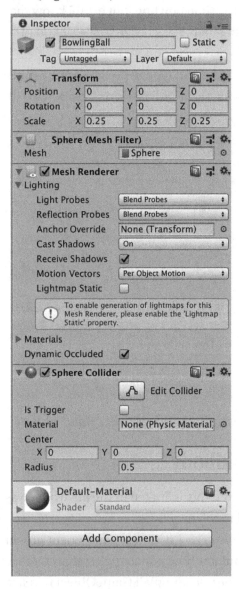

Figure 5-10. *Adding a Component*

In the Add Component menu, there is a search bar. In the search bar, type in Rigid and select the Rigidbody component (Figure 5-11).

Figure 5-11. *Searching for the RigidBody Component*

The default settings of the Rigidbody Component are pretty good, but a mass of 1 kilogram is a bit light for a bowling ball. Let's set the Mass to 5, as 5 kg, is about right for a bowling ball. The other settings are fine for now (but we may have to adjust these later on after testing). Figure 5-12 shows the settings for the BowlingBall.

Figure 5-12. *The BowlingBall RigidBody settings*

In Figure 5-12, we can see that our BowlingBall has a component called Sphere Collider. A Collider Component provides our GameObject with a collision shape. In this case, when we created our Sphere GameObject, a Sphere-shaped collider was also added. The Collider components will dictate at what point a GameObject will collide. But, a collider does not determine how it will collide (bounce, slide, or not move at all). To set how the GameObject reacts to a Collision, we need to add a Physics Material. To get the physics materials, we need to download the Unity Standard Assets package from the Unity Store (we could have added this to our Project when we first created it). There are other Physics materials available in the Asset Store, some of these are free, and others you need to pay for.

Opening the Asset Store

Select the Asset Store view tab to show the Asset Store (Figure 5-13). In the search bar, type in Standard Assets. If you want to add the filter to only show free assets, that will limit the search results (Figure 5-14).

Figure 5-13. *The Unity Asset Store view*

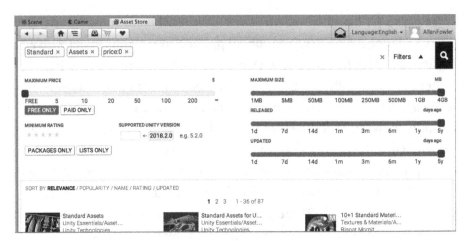

Figure 5-14. *Searching for Standard Assets (Free)*

Select the Standard Assets package and this will open the information screen on this package (Figure 5-15). Select Install (or Update if you have installed this when you created the Project).

Figure 5-15. *The package information screen*

After a few minutes (depending on your download speed), Unity will open the Import Unity package Menu (Figure 5-16). While we don't need all of these assets, let's just select Import (we can always delete anything we don't need or want later on).

Figure 5-16. *The Unity Import Package screen*

After a few minutes, the package will be imported, and you will see some additional assets in your Project folder (Figure 5-17).

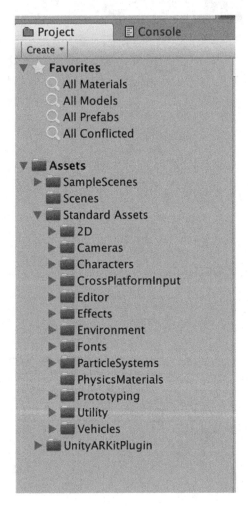

Figure 5-17. *The Unity Standard Assets Package in the project folder*

If we select the PhysicsMaterials folder, we can see that now we have a selection of PhysicsMaterials to select from (Figure 5-18).

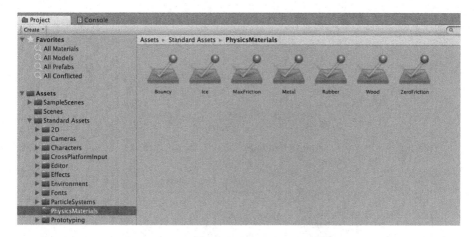

Figure 5-18. *The Unity Standard Assets Package PhysicsMaterials folder*

PhysicsMaterials

The Standard Assets Package has given us a base of PhysicsMaterials to use. However, none of them provide the best PhysicsMaterial for our BowlingBall. For now, let's use the Wood PhysicsMaterial. As we may need to use this material for another part of the game, let's duplicate it. From the main menu select Edit ➤ Duplicate (or Command+D). Now in the Project folder, select the duplicate PhysicsMaterial (Wood 1) and rename it Ball (Figure 5-19).

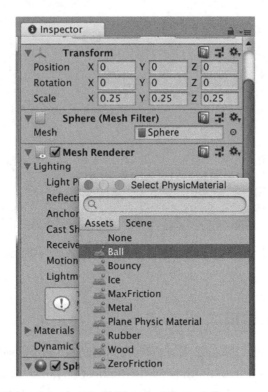

Figure 5-19. *Selecting the Ball PhysicsMaterial*

Now in select the BowlingBall GameObject and in the Hierarchy, select the small gear next to the properties box of the Material property in the Sphere Collider component and then select the Ball PhysicsMaterial we just created (technically duplicated) (Figure 5-19). In the Project tab double-click the Ball PhysicsMaterial to set the physics properties. Set the Dynamic Friction to 1, the Static Fiction to 1, the Bounciness to 0, the Friction Combine to Maximum, and the Bounce Combine to Minimum (Figure 5-20).

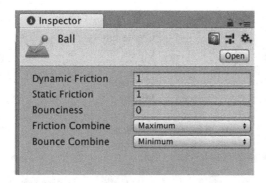

Figure 5-20. *Setting the Ball PhysicsMaterial Properties*

Creating a (Temporary) Plane

If we were to test our game right now, we would see our ball drop (and never stop). Although, we are going to use real-world surfaces, for now, let's install a temporary Plane GameObject to help us test our game in the Game view.

From the main menu, select GameObject ➤ 3D Object ➤ Plane (Figure 5-21). Select the Plane in the Hierarchy and rename it Plane(t). If you look in the Scene view, you will note that the plane has been created at the Origin and, as a result, cuts through our BowlingBall. Let's reposition our Plane(t) so it sits just under the BowlingBall (Figure 5-22).

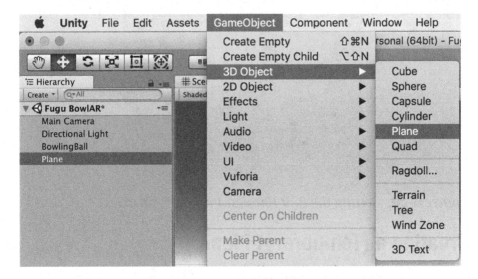

Figure 5-21. *Creating a Plane*

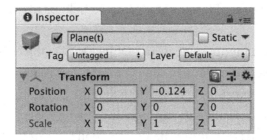

Figure 5-22. *The Plane(t) Transform settings*

If we look at the Scene view, the color of Plane(t) and the BowlingBall are the same. Let's change the color of the Plane(t). In the Project folder search for Material (Figure 5-23), you will see there are several assets that we can use; I am going to use the BallMaterial for the Plane(t). There are several ways of changing the Material properties, but the easiest is to select and drag and drop the BallMaterial onto the Plane(t) in the Scene view (Figure 5-24).

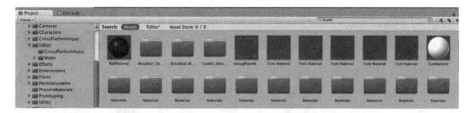

Figure 5-23. *Searching for the BallMaterial*

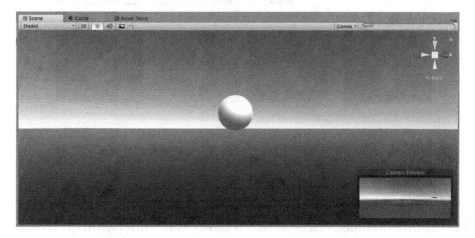

Figure 5-24. *The Plane(t) with the BallMaterial*

Now, let's add some Pins (or Skittles depending on where you're from). If we look in the Asset Store for Bowling Pins, we will find that the only options are Paid Assets. However, our good friends at Google have a fantastic library of AR and VR assets on https://poly.google.com/. Open this site with your favorite browser and search for Pins. You will find there are a couple of great choices (Figure 5-25).

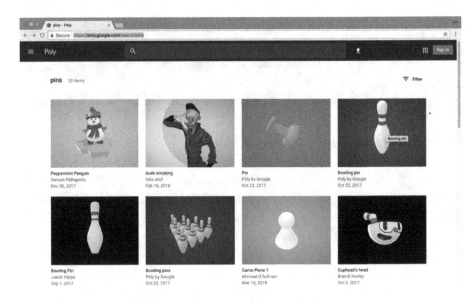

Figure 5-25. *Searching for Pins in Google Poly*

Select the Pins you want to use; I am going to use the Bowling Pin from Poly by Google. If we check the license, we can see that it is available under the Creative Commons License, which allows us to use it (see `https://creativecommons.org/` for more detail). Select the Download link and choose OBJ to download this image. While you're on the Google Poly page, check out some of the amazing content.

Importing an OBJ file to Unity

When the file has finished downloading, open the folder it was saved to and right-click (or double-click) to Unzip the folder (Figure 5-26). In the folder, you will see that there is an OBJ file (which is what we need). Now in Unity select from the main menu Assets ➤ Import New Assets and browse to the Unzipped folder with the Pin OBJ file and select the OBJ file and select Import.

Figure 5-26. *Unzipping the Bowling_Pin.obj folder*

After Unity has finished importing this asset, it should appear in the Assets folder (Figure 5-27). I am going to create a new folder to keep any imported Art that I might use. If you don't find this asset in the Assets folder, be sure to search for it in the Project View tab.

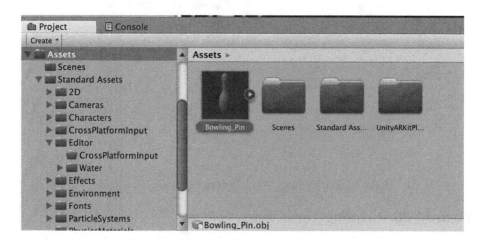

Figure 5-27. *The Bowling_Pin Asset in the Asset Folder*

Creating a new Project Folder

To create a new folder in the Project view, in the Project Folder right-click and select from the menu and select Create ➤ Folder (Figure 5-28).

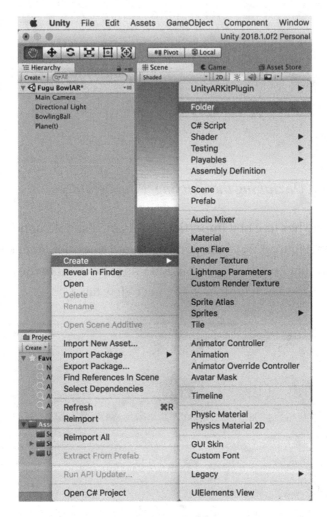

Figure 5-28. *Creating a new Project Folder*

Unity will create the folder in the Assets Project folder, and now we need to name it and drag and drop our Bowling_Pin asset to this folder. I am going to name this folder Art Assets (Figure 5-29).

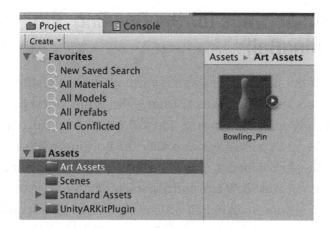

Figure 5-29. *The Art Assets folder with the Bowling_Pin asset*

Adding the Bowling_Pin to the Scene

With the Bowling_Pin asset selected, drag it to the Hierarchy (or the Scene view) (Figure 5-30). You will note that once again, we need to Transform the position and scale of this GameObject.

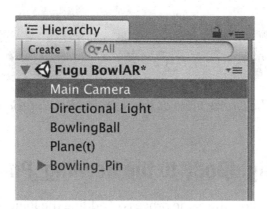

Figure 5-30. *The Bowling_Pin in the Hierarchy*

Transform Settings for the Bowling_Pin and BowlingBall

Let's first scale our Bowling_Pin, as it is currently set at a scale of 1,1,1. However, the correct dimensions 121mm wide (at the widest point) and 380 mm tall. Let's scale the Bowling_Pin to 0.4,0.4,0.4. It's not to perfect scale but looks pretty good. Let's also scale the BowlingBall to a relative scale. According to Wikipedia, A bowling ball may have a circumference between 67.83 cm and 68.59 cm, and a diameter in the range of 21.59 cm to 21.83 cm. Let's set our BowlingBall scale to 0.1,0.1,0.1. It's not quite to scale but good enough for now. Figure 5-31 shows my BowlingBall next to my BowlingPin. They look pretty good (to me).

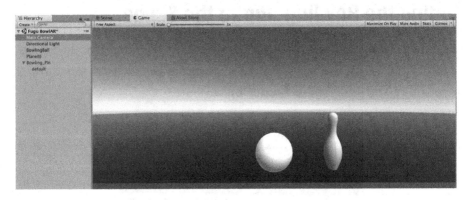

Figure 5-31. *The Game view of the rescaled BowlingBall and Bowling_Pin*

Adding a RigidBody to the Bowling_Pin

We are going to follow the same process of adding the RigidBody and PhysicsMaterial to the Bowling_Pin as we did with the BowlingBall. With the Bowling_Pin selected in the Hierarchy, in the Inspector, select Add Component and search for and add a RigidBody component (Figure 5-32).

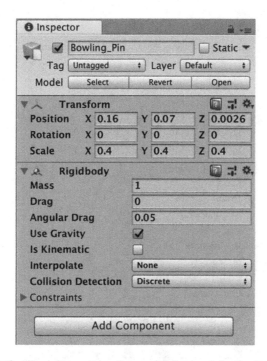

Figure 5-32. *The Bowling_Pin GameObject with the RigidBody component*

Adding a Collider to the Bowling_Pin

If we look at the Inspector of our Bowling_Pin, you will note that there is no Collider. That's because it did not come with a Collider as it is a non-convex shape. We are going to Add a Collider, so we can add a PhysicsMaterial. With the Bowling_Pin selected, in the Inspector, select Add Component and search for a mesh (Figure 5-33).

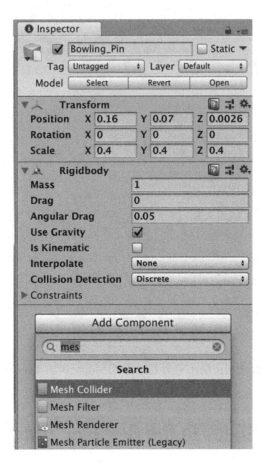

Figure 5-33. *Searching for the Mesh Collider component*

Now, select and add the Mesh Collider component. The Mesh Collider will enable us to create a mesh that will surround a Game Object. In the Mesh Collider component, we just added, there is a properties box for us to set the type of mesh we want to use. The mesh collider component enables us to add a mesh that is a convex shape (cylinder, cube, sphere, or plane).

As our Bowling_Pin is closest to a cylinder shape, let's search for a cylinder mesh and add this to the Bowling_Pin GameObject. Select the small gear to the right of the properties box of the Mesh settings of the Mesh Collider and search for Cylinder (Figure 5-34). Select the Cylinder mesh to set this as the shape of the Mesh Collider (Figure 5-35). Also note, I have set the Rigidbody component as a Kinematic.

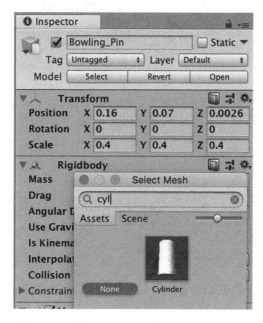

Figure 5-34. *Searching for the Cylinder Mesh*

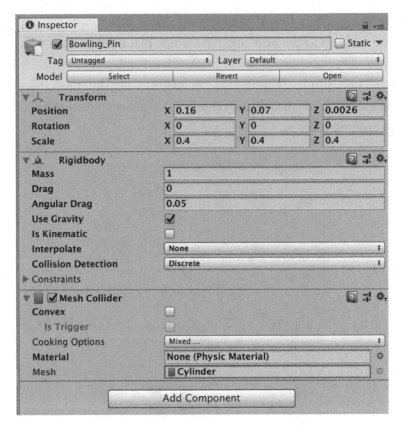

Figure 5-35. *The Cylinder Mesh set as the Mesh Collider*

Adding a PhysicsMaterial to the Bowling_Pin

Just like we did for the BowlingBall, we need to add a physics property to set how our bowling pin reacts to collisions. As the physics properties of a bowling pin are similar to a bowling ball, let's duplicate the Ball PhysicsMaterial and rename it BowlingPin and change the settings.

First, select and duplicate the ball PhysicsMaterial and name it BowlingPin (Figure 5-36). Select the BowlingPin PhysicsMaterial and change the settings to the following; Dynamic Friction = 1, Static Friction = 1, Bounciness = 0.5, Friction Combine = Maximum, Bounce Combine = Minimum (Figure 5-37).

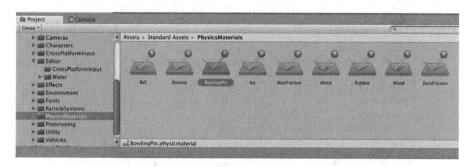

Figure 5-36. *The BowlingPin PhysicsMaterial*

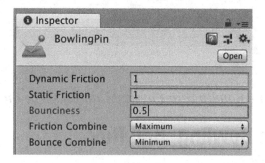

Figure 5-37. *The BowlingPin PhysicsMaterial settings*

Now add the BowlingPin PhysicsMaterial to the BowlingPin GameObject Mesh Collider (Figure 5-38).

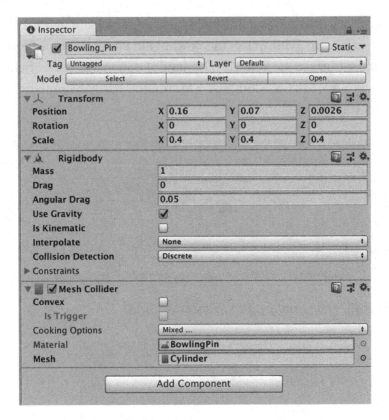

Figure 5-38. *The BowlingPin PhysicsMaterial set as the Material*

Making the Bowling_Ball Roll

To make our Bowling_Ball roll based on the Player input, we need to create a script. As I have already indicated, this is not an Introductory Programming book, so I won't spend a lot of time going into the purpose of each line of code. There may be some important parts of the code that I feel are worth noting, and I will include comments in the Script to explain the purpose of those lines of code. Let's first make a folder to keep all our Scripts in. In the Project view, right-click and select Create ➤ Folder. Let's name this Scripts (Figure 5-39). You may want to call this folder something really funny or cool, but it's good practice to use a file-naming convention so that if someone else needs to edit or modify your game, they can easily identify where to find the assets in your project.

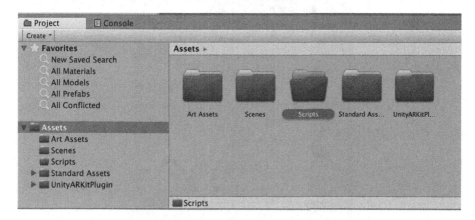

Figure 5-39. *The Scripts folder*

For now, we are going to create a script that will enable us to test the user input in Unity. As a result, we are going to get our BowlingBall GameObject to move based on Keyboard (or Mouse) input. We will change this later on so that the input is based on Touch, Tap, or Swipe. In the Hierarchy, select our BowlingBall GameObject and select Add Component. In the Add Component, select New Script (Figure 5-40). First, let's name this Script PlayerController and select Create and Add. This option enables us to both create the Script and Add it to our BowlingBall GameObject. Unity will place this Script in the Assets folder. We need to select and move (drag and drop) this script to our Scripts menu (Figure 5-41).

Figure 5-40. *Adding a New Script Component*

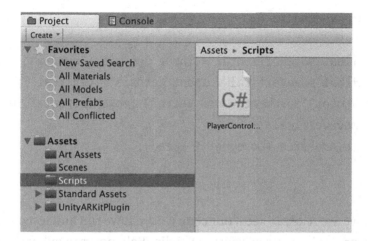

Figure 5-41. *The PlayerController Script added to the Scripts folder*

Editing the PlayerController Script

Now let's edit the PlayerController Script. If you select the PlayerController Script, you can see the code for this asset in the Inspector. Let's edit this code. Double-click the PlayerController script and this will open your default IDE. I am using Visual Studio. Enter the following code as shown in Listing 5-1.

Listing 5-1. The PlayerController Script

```
using UnityEngine;
using System.Collections;
public class PlayerController : MonoBehaviour {
    public float speed;
    private Rigidbody rb;
    void Start ()
    {
        rb = GetComponent<Rigidbody>();
    }
```

```
void FixedUpdate ()
{
    float moveHorizontal = Input.GetAxis ("Horizontal");
    float moveVertical = Input.GetAxis ("Vertical");
    Vector3 movement = new Vector3 (moveHorizontal, 0.0f,
    moveVertical);
    rb.AddForce (movement * speed);
}
}
```

Now we are ready to see if our code works. If we run and test our game when we press either arrow key, the BowlingBall moves in either direction (which is good, well kind of, as we only really need the ball to move in one direction). However, you will note that the collider on the Bowling_Pin is too big, and the collisions are not realistic. Now, we could edit this collider, but we are going to create our own collider.

Creating Our Own Collider

To create our own Collider, we are going to use a bit of game design magic (also known as faking it). To do this, in the Hierarchy select the Bowling_Pin GameObject and in the Mesh Collider Component select the small gear and right-click and remove the current Collider (Figure 5-42). Now from the Main menu, select GameObject ➤ 3D Object ➤ Capsule (Figure 5-43).

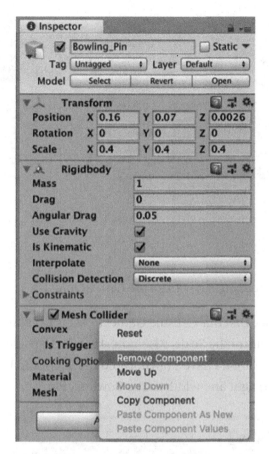

Figure 5-42. *The PlayerController Script added to the Scripts folder*

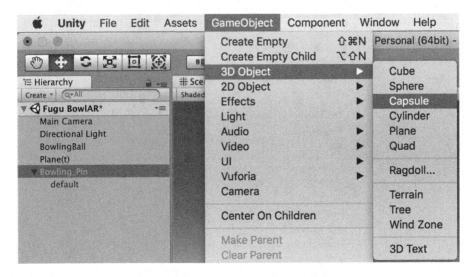

Figure 5-43. *Creating a 3D Capsule GameObject*

You will notice that our Capsule GameObject is a bit big and therefore, we need to Transform the Scale. Also note, that the Capsule has its own Collider. In Figure 5-44, I have Transformed the Scale and Position, so it is about the same height and width as the Bowling_Pin.

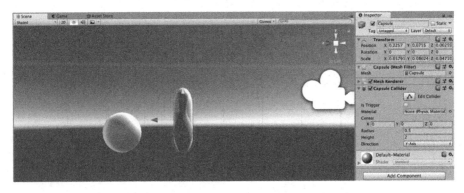

Figure 5-44. *The Rescaled and repositioned Capsule*

Now we add a PhysicsMaterial to our Capsule, so that it can respond to the force of our BowlingBall. For now, let's use the BowlingPin PhysicsMaterial. With the Capsule selected, in the Inspector, select the small gear next to the Material properties box and right-click and add the BowlingPin PhysicsMaterial (Figure 5-45).

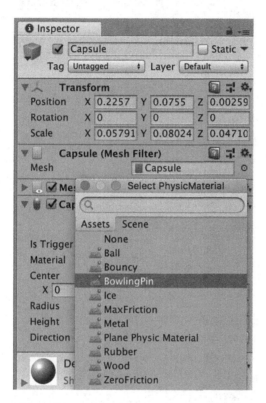

Figure 5-45. *Adding the BowlingPin Physics Material*

With the Capsule GameObject selected, let's give this a meaningful name. I'm going to go with BowlingPinCollider.

Now that we have moved the BowlingPinCollider so it totally covers the Bowling_Pin GameObject, the next step is to make it invisible to the player. To make the BowlingPinCollider GameObject invisible to the player, in the

Hierarchy select the BowlingPinCollider GameObject and in the Inspector, in the Mesh Renderer Component, select the gear to the right and select Remove Component (Figure 5-46).

Figure 5-46. *Removing the Mesh Renderer Component*

Remembering the Parents

You might recall earlier in Chapter, I discussed Parents and Children in software development. We are going to make the Bowling_Pin a Child of the BowlingPinCollider. This way, whatever happens to the BowlingPinCollider will also happen to the Bowling_Pin.

Making a Parent

Becoming a parent was one of the most exciting and intimidating experiences of my life. Fortunately, Unity makes the process of creating a Parent GameObject a lot less intimidating (and probably a lot less exciting as well). To make our BowlingPinCollider a Parent of the Bowling_Pin GameObject, we simply drag the Bowling_Pin GameObject to the BowlingPinCollider and it will become a child of the BowlingPinCollider (Figure 5-47). If only life was that easy.

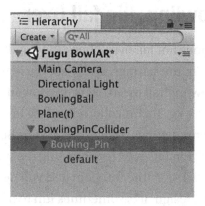

Figure 5-47. The BowlingPinCollider as a Parent of the Bowling_Pin

Now let's test our work to see if our Collider does what it should. Phew, my collider worked (Figure 5-48). But the BowlingPinCollider Parent and the Child Bowling_Pin still do not fall over. I'll be really honest with you, this pretty much reflects my bowling ability in real life. However, I think the players are going to get a bit frustrated if they can't knock over the bowling pin. So, let's make a couple of changes to make this a bit more realistic.

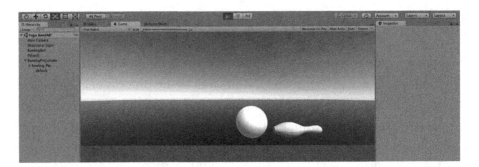

Figure 5-48. *The Game view of the collision*

Making the Bowling_Pin fall Over

If your Bowling_Pin does not fall over, check the Rigidbody Components on each GameObject. In my settings, I have set the Mass of the RigidBody Component of the BowlingBall to 5 (that is the BowlingBall is 5 kg). I have set the Bowling_Pin to 1 kg. Technically, a Bowling Pin should weigh 1.6 kg. So, I'm going to leave my settings as they are. If your BowlingBall does not make the Bowling_Pin fall over, try adjusting the weight. The player will never physically pick up either of them and will never know the exact weight. Plus, in Game Design, it is sometimes fun to overemphasize reality.

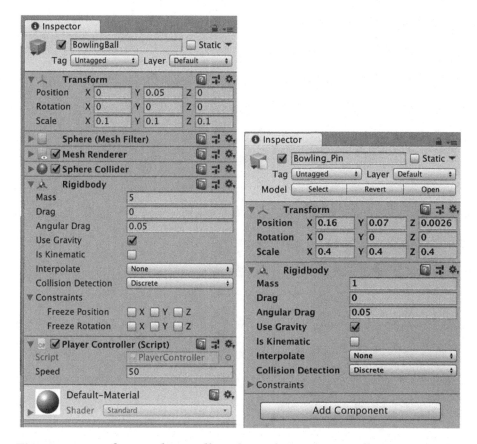

Figure 5-49. The BowlingBall and Bowling_Pin Rigidbody Components

Summary

In this chapter, we have created a new scene and added GameObjects. We have added RigidBody Components and PhysicsMaterials. We have successfully tested out our game to see if it works in the GameView. In the next chapter, we will test the game in AR to see how it looks.

CHAPTER 6

Introducing Touch

Testing the Game in AR

In the last chapter we were able to test our Game in the Unity Game View; now, let's see what the game will look like in AR. With the FuguBowlAR Game open in Unity, let's add the Unity AR Camera Manager to our Main Camera. In the Hierarchy select the Main Camera and then in the Inspector, select Add Component (Figure 6-1). In the Add Component search bar, search for Camera and select the Unity AR Camera Manager (Figure 6-2).

© Allan Fowler 2019
A. Fowler, *Beginning iOS AR Game Development*,
https://doi.org/10.1007/978-1-4842-3618-5_6

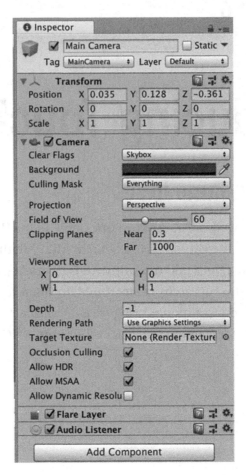

Figure 6-1. *Add Component*

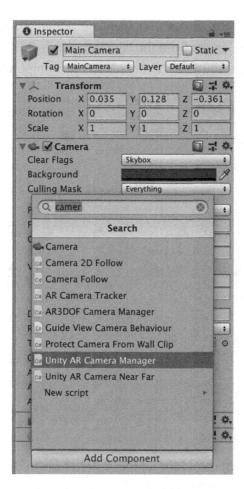

Figure 6-2. *Adding the Unity AR Camera Manager Component*

With the Unity AR, Camera Manager Component added, now select and drag the Main Camera from the Hierarchy and add this to the Camera properties box of the Unity AR Camera Manager component (Figure 6-3).

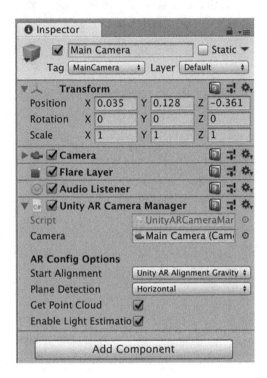

Figure 6-3. *Adding the Main Camera to the Camera Properties*

Now with the Unity AR Camera Manager component added to the Main Camera, let's preview what the game will look like in the Game view, using the Unity AR Kit Remote App we installed on our device. First, connect your device to your Mac, and then start the Unity AR Kit Remote App on your device. In Unity, select the Console view and select Editor and then select your device (Figure 6-4). Now, select the Play button from the Unity Game view and then in the game view, select (Figure 6-5). You should see the game now working in the Game view of Unity (Figure 6-6).

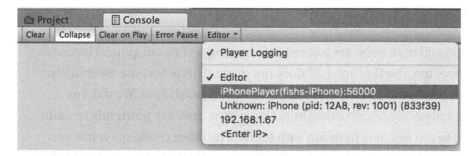

Figure 6-4. *Connecting to the iPhonePlayer*

Figure 6-5. *Start the Remote ARKit Session*

Figure 6-6. *Game view of the AR version*

Some Challenges

You will note there are a couple of challenges with our game. First, as expected, the Bowling Ball does not move. This is because we initially set the BowlingBall code to respond to keyboard input. We did this intentionally because the Unity Game view does not (currently) enable us to test out user iteration with touch. The other challenge is that our Plane(t) is still visible. Let's first disable the Plane(t). I don't want to delete it right now, because I might want to use it for testing later on.

Disabling the Plane(t)

Disabling the Plane(t) GameObject is relatively straightforward. In the Hierarchy view, select the Plane(t) GameObject and then in the Inspector, select the check box to the left of the GameObject name (Figure 6-7). You will immediately see that the Plane(t) GameObject is no longer visible. The impact of this will be clearly visible when we test our game.

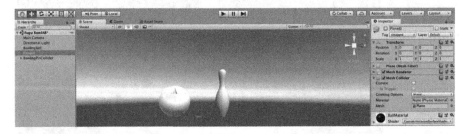

Figure 6-7. *The Plane(t) GameObject disabled*

Testing

To test our game, there are two ways. The first and most efficient way would be to test it in the Game view. To do this, we need to disable the Unity AR Camera Manager Component that we added to the camera. Select the Main Camera, and then deselect the check box to the left of the file name (Figure 6-8).

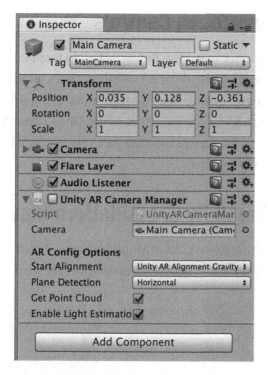

Figure 6-8. *The Unity Camera Manager deselected*

Now press the play button, and you should see the BowlingBall and the Bowling_Pin fall to infinity (and quite possibly beyond infinity).

The second way to test our game would be leaving the Unity AR Camera manager selected and connecting our device to our Mac and then running the Unity AR Kit Remote App on our device. Then in the Console tab, select our device and select the play button in Unity. After selecting the Play button, you will be prompted with the Start ARKit Remote Session prompt, and the preview of the game will appear in the Unity Game tab. However, once again, the BowlingBall and Bowling_Pin GameObject's fall and keep on falling.

Implementing Touch Controls

Now we are going to try to get the Bowling_Ball to respond to the user touching the screen on their device. Over the years, Unity has made a number of changes on how to manage user input using a device with touch controls. In my example, I am going to use the Unity CrossPlatformInput Manager, which was the way to manage multiple forms of input (including touch), when I wrote this book.

Importing the Unity CrossPlatformInput Package

Let's import the Unity CrossPlatformInput package. From the menu, select Assets ➤ Import Package ➤ CrossPlatformInput (Figure 6-9).

Figure 6-9. Import the Unity CrossPlatformInput Package

The file will download and, when complete, will open the Import Unity Package utility (Figure 6-10). While we don't need all of this content, let's select Import. The Import Unity Package utility will now add the complete package.

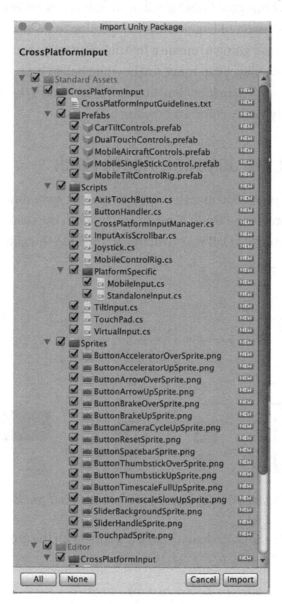

Figure 6-10. *Importing the Unity CrossPlatformInput Package*

Adding Touch Controls

Now we are going to create a graphical user interface (or GUI) so that the player can control the bowling ball by touching the screen. As we are creating an AR version of Fugu Bowl, we are going to need to do things a bit different. We are going to create a Joystick controller and put this on the screen so that the player can move the bowling ball in both the X- and Y- axes. Now, I don't do a lot of bowling, but even I know that this is not how we would typically control a bowling ball.

Download the Joystick Asset Pack

First, we need some good assets, so let's go and get something from the Unity Asset Store. In the Unity Asset store Tab, from the search bar, search for Joystick (Figure 6-11). If you want to add the Free Only filter, that might save you some time.

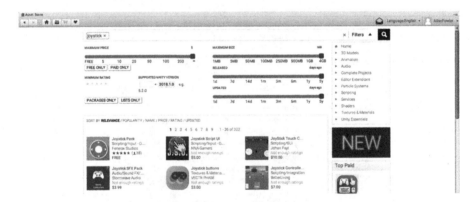

Figure 6-11. *Searching for the Joystick Pack asset pack*

Select the Joy Stick Pack asset pack (the one with the green icon) and select Import (Figure 6-12).

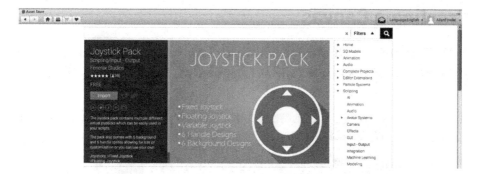

Figure 6-12. *Importing the Joy Stick Asset Pack*

From the Unity Import Package Utility, select Import All (Figure 6-13).

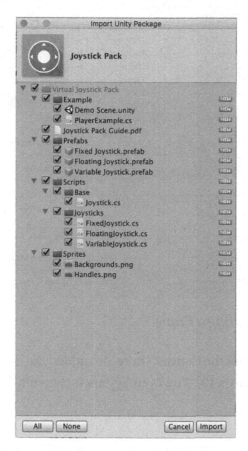

Figure 6-13. *Import Unity Package Utility*

Creating a Canvas

In Unity to create a UI, we need to create a canvas. In the Hierarchy, right-click and select UI ➤ Canvas (Figure 6-14).

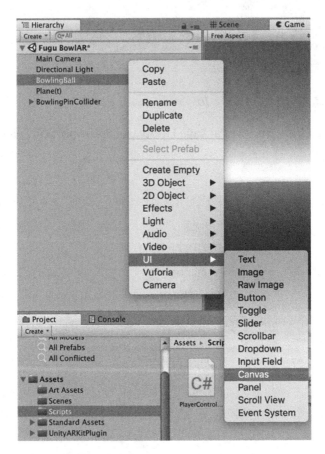

Figure 6-14. *Creating a Canvas*

When we created the Canvas, Unity also added the EventSystem GameObject (Figure 6-15). The EventSystem is currently how Unity handles UI events.

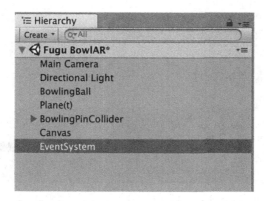

Figure 6-15. *The EventSystem GameObject added to the Hierarchy*

Adding the Joystick UI to the Canvas

Now we are going to move the Fixed Joystick Prefab from the Virtual Joystick Folder in the Project tab to the Canvas. To do this, in the Project tab, search for Fixed (Figure 6-16) and select the Fixed Joystick Prefab and then drag this to the Canvas folder in the Hierarchy (Figure 6-17). Once added, you can actually playtest the Joystick to see it in action. It won't move our BowlingBall; we need to add a script to do this.

Figure 6-16. *Searching for the Fixed Joystick Prefab*

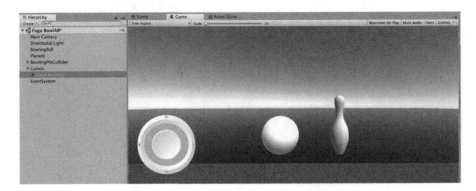

Figure 6-17. *The Fixed Joystick Prefab added to the Canvas*

Adding a Script

In the Hierarchy, select the BowlingBall GameObject and in the Inspector, disable or remove the Player Controller Script. To remove the Player Controller Script Component, in the Inspector right-click the small gear to the right of the Player Controller Script Component and select Remove Component (Figure 6-18).

Figure 6-18. *Removing the Player Controller Script Component*

Now in the Project tab, search for and select the PlayerExample Script (Figure 6-19) and drag this script onto the BowlingBall Game Object (Figure 6-20).

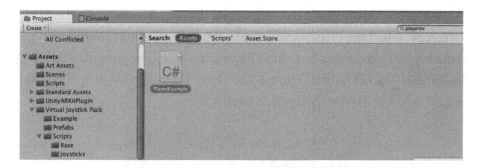

Figure 6-19. *Searching for the PlayerExample Script*

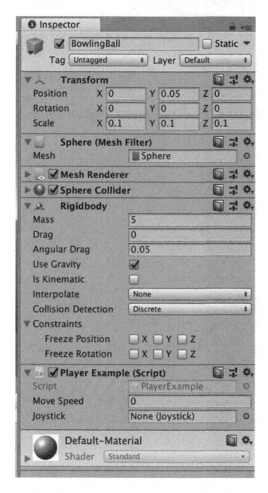

Figure 6-20. *The Player Example Script added to the BowlingBall*

Before you do anything else, make sure the speed is set. From the Hierarchy, select the FixedJoysick GameObject (Figure 6-21) and drag this to the Joystick properties box of the Player Example Component of the BowlingBall GameObject (Figure 6-22). I have set the Speed to 5. This may be a bit fast, but we can change this later on.

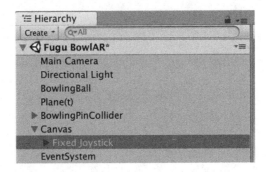

Figure 6-21. *Selecting the Fixed Joystick GameObject*

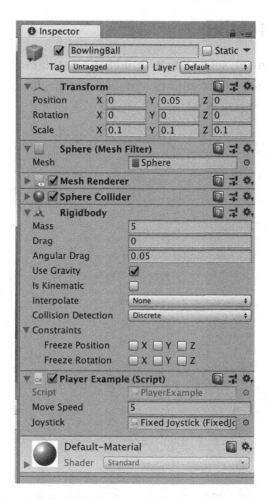

Figure 6-22. *Setting the Move Speed and Joystick properties*

Testing

Now we can test our Virtual Joystick and see if it works. First, I highly recommend you test it in the Game tab. This will save you exporting the build to your device and finding that it does not work (however, just because the game will work in Unity, this does not always mean it will work on our device).

If the game works in Unity, now test it on a device.

On Device Testing

From the Unity menu, select File ➤ Build Settings (Figure 6-23). In the Build Settings select player settings and, in the Inspector, change the version number (Figure 6-24).

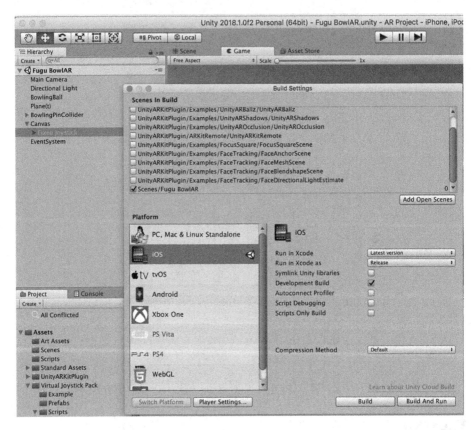

Figure 6-23. *Build Settings*

Figure 6-24. *Player Settings*

Success

After we select Build and Run from the Build menu, Unity will compile the code and open Xcode. After the code has compiled in Xcode, the game will be installed on your iOS device. In Figure 6-25, I have successfully created the App and the Virtual Joystick works. As noted, the BowlingBall speed is too fast, but for now, let's leave it as it is.

Figure 6-25. *FuguBowlAR on my iPhone*

CHAPTER 7

Adding Plane Detection and Point Clouds

Now we are going to add the Generated Planes to our game, which will help the ARKit camera track the movement of the device.

Creating the Generated Planes GameObject

Just like we did in Chapter 3, create an empty GameObject. From the file menu, select GameObject ➤ Empty (Figure 7-1).

© Allan Fowler 2019
A. Fowler, *Beginning iOS AR Game Development*,
https://doi.org/10.1007/978-1-4842-3618-5_7

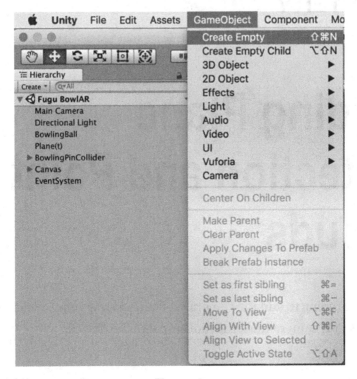

Figure 7-1. *Creating an empty GameObject*

With the GameObject selected, in the Inspector, name this Created Planes (Figure 7-2).

Figure 7-2. *Naming GameObject Created Planes*

Now we need to add a component. Select the Add Component button in the Created Planes Inspector; and in the search bar, search for the Unity AR Generated Plane script (Figure 7-3).

Figure 7-3. *Searching for the Unity AR Generated Plane script*

With the Unity AR Generated Plane script included in the Created Planes GameObject, in the Plane Prefab setting of the Unity AR Generated Plane script, select the small gear to the right of the option box and search for and select the DebugPlanePrefab (Figure 7-4).

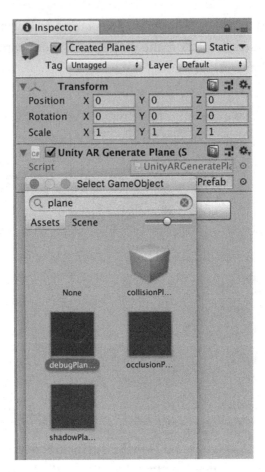

Figure 7-4. *Searching for the debugPlanePrefab*

Creating the Point Cloud GameObject

Creat an empty GameObject (Figure 7-5). With the Empty GameObject selected in the Inspector, rename it Point Cloud. Now add a component. In the search bar, search for the Unity Point Cloud Particle Example and add this to the Point Cloud GameObject (Figure 7-6).

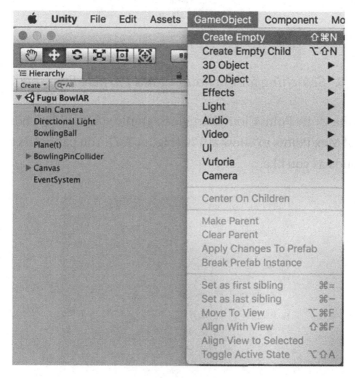

Figure 7-5. *Creating an empty GameObject*

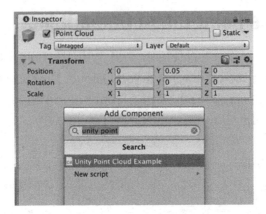

Figure 7-6. *Searching for the Point Cloud Particle Example*

With the Unity Point Cloud Particle Example script added, now set the number of Max Points to Show at 120 (Figure 7-7). You can set as many Point Clouds as you like.

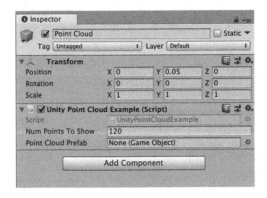

Figure 7-7. *Setting the Max Points to Show*

Now add a Point Cloud Particle Prefab to the Point Cloud Prefab properties box. Select the small gear to the right of the Point Cloud Prefab properties box and then search for the Point Cloud Prefab (Figure 7-8). Select and drag the PointCloudPrefab to the Point Cloud Particle Prefab box in the Point Cloud Particle Example script (Figure 7-9).

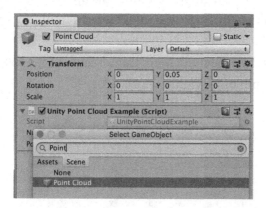

Figure 7-8. *Searching for the PointCloud Prefab*

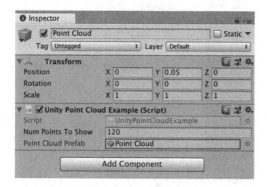

Figure 7-9. *The PointCloudPrefab set as the Point Cloud Prefab*

Setting Up the Main Camera

You might recall that in Chapter 3, we needed to set up the game for AR. The first thing we need to do is change the settings of the Main Camera. If you remember how to do this, you can skip this section. However, I will provide a guide to setting this up for those readers who read Chapter 3 some time ago and might need a reminder on how we set this up,

In the Hierarchy, select the Main Camera and in the Inspector, set the Clear Flags to Depth only (Figure 7-10).

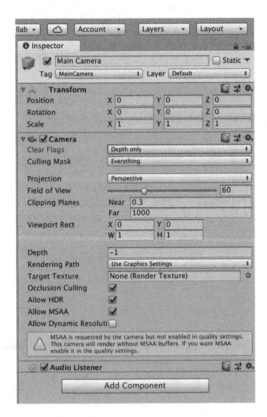

Figure 7-10. *Set the Clear Flags to Depth only*

With the Main Camera selected, in the Inspector select Add Component. Now search for and add the Unity AR Video Script (Figure 7-11).

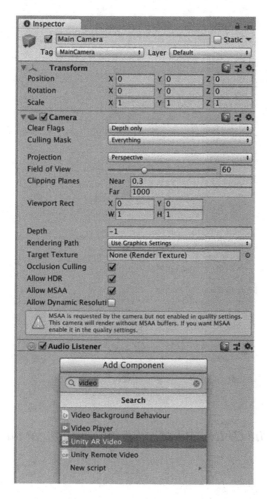

Figure 7-11. *Searching for the Unity AR Video Script component*

Now select the Unity AR Video Script (single, left mouse click) and this component should be added to the Main Camera (Figure 7-12).

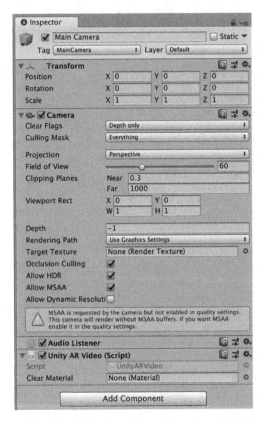

Figure 7-12. *The Unity AR Video Script component added to the main camera*

Setting the Unity AR Video Script Clear Materials

On the right of the properties box of the Unity AR Video Script component, there is a small gear (Figure 7-12); select this gear, and search for the YUV material (Figure 7-13).

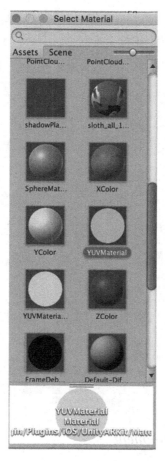

Figure 7-13. *Selecting the YUV material for the Clear Material*

Adding the Unity AR Camera Manager

With the Main Camera still selected, in the Inspector, select Add Component
(Figure 7-14); now search for AR Camera Manager (Figure 7-15), and now
add it to the Main Camera.

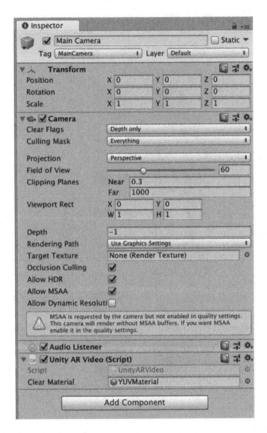

Figure 7-14. *Add Component*

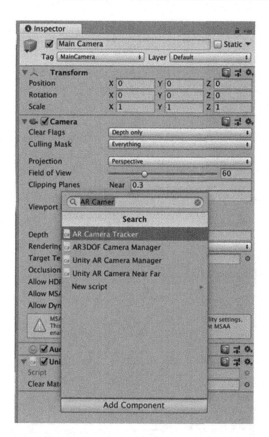

Figure 7-15. *Searching for the Unity AR Camera Tracker*

Now add the Main Camera as the Tracked Camera. To add the Main
Camera to the Camera Properties of the Unity AR Camera Manager, select
the Main Camera from the Hierarchy and drag this to the Tracked Camera
properties of the Unity AR Camera Manager (Figure 7-16).

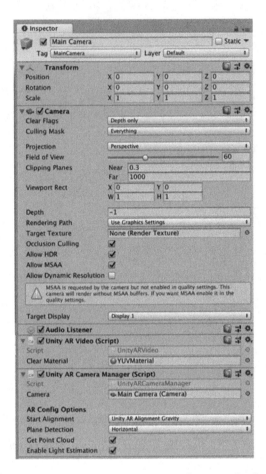

Figure 7-16. *Setting the Main Camera as the Tracked Camera*

Adding the Unity Remote Connection

To test our game in the Game tab, we also need to add the Unity Remote
Connection to our Hierarchy. In the Project Tab, search for a Prefab called
ARKitRemoteConnection (Figure 7-17).

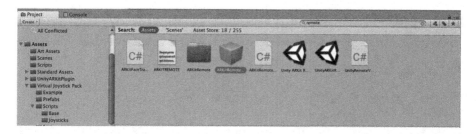

Figure 7-17. *Searching for the UnityARKitRemoteConnection Prefab*

Select this Prefab and add it to the Scene (drag it to the Hierarchy) (Figure 7-18).

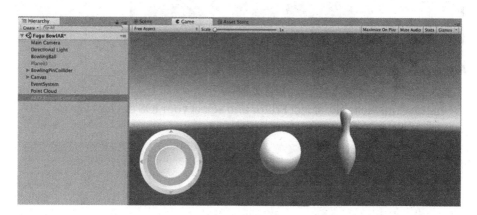

Figure 7-18. *The UnityARKitRemoteConnection in the Scene*

Now we need to open the ARKitRemote on our iOS device. First, connect your iOS device to your development computer. In Unity, select the Game tab and press the Play button. Unity will prompt you to connect to the player in the console menu (Figure 7-19).

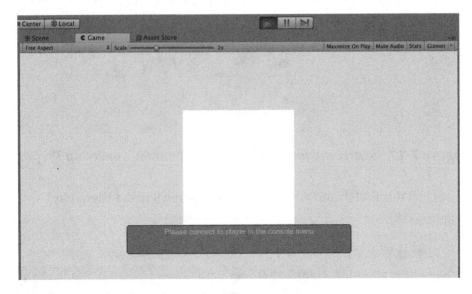

Figure 7-19. *Unity connect to player message*

In the Console table, select Editor and select your iOS device (Figure 7-20).

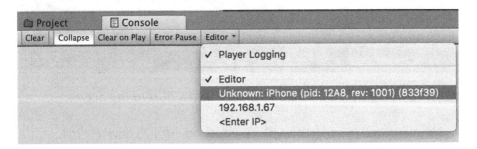

Figure 7-20. *Selecting the iOS device in the Console menu*

Then Unity will prompt you to Start Remote ARKit Session (Figure 7-21). Click the icon on the Game screen in Unity and your application can now run on your iOS device.

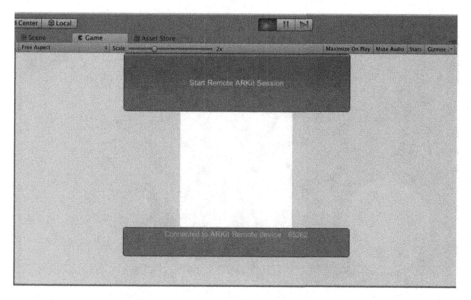

Figure 7-21. *Start Remote ARKit Session prompt*

In Figure 7-22 you can see that I have successfully been able to view the Hello WorldAR App on my iPhone and see the Scene in Unity. If you move your device, you should see the Camera move in the Unity Scene tab and the picture change in the Game tab. I would like to point out that it's going to be a bit slow (lag), but the ARKitRemote is currently the best way to test Unity AR development for iOS.

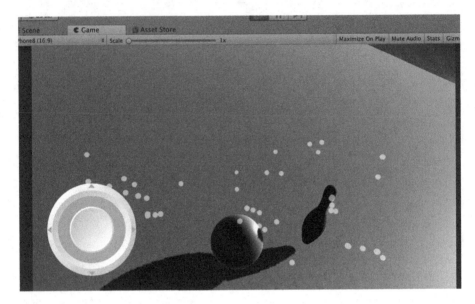

Figure 7-22. *The Game View*

Houston, We Have a Problem...

If you get a similar result as I have in Figure 7-23, don't panic! The scene is rendering in real time. The BowlingBall and Bowling_Pin are being rendered and so is the Virtual Joystick. We can see the Point Clouds. But... the Pane(t) is still visible.

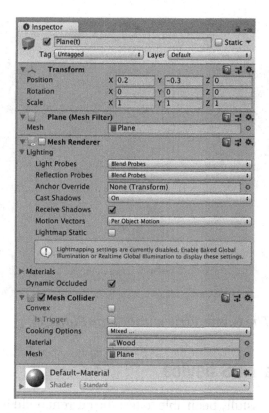

Figure 7-23. *The Mesh Renderer de-selected*

To fix this challenge, we are going to disable the Mesh Renderer Component of our Plane(t). To do this, in the Hierarchy, select the Plane(t) GameObject and in the Inspector, deselect the Mesh Renderer (Figure 7-24). To do this, left mouse click the check mark in the check box to the left of the Mesh Renderer Component.

Now retest your build and see the result. Your result should be similar to mine (Figure 7-24).

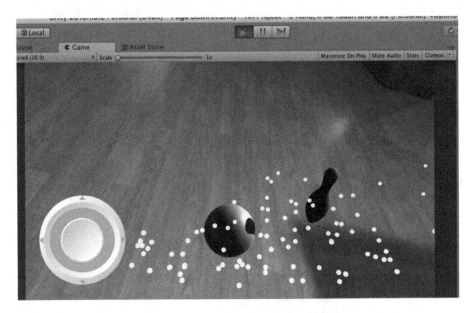

Figure 7-24. *The Game View without the Plane(t)*

Testing on an iOS device

As we have successfully been able to test the current build in the Game View, now would be a good time to see if this works on our device.

From the Main Menu, select from the Main Menu, File ➤ Build Settings (Figure 7-25). Make sure you have selected iOS as the Platform, and the Development Build check box is selected. Also, be sure to check that you are building the correct scene (Figure 7-26). In the Build Settings Menu, select Player Settings and in the Inspector make sure that the Other Settings options are set correctly. I have set my version to version 3.0. However, you might want to use a different version number (Figure 7-27).

Figure 7-25. *Selecting the Build Settings*

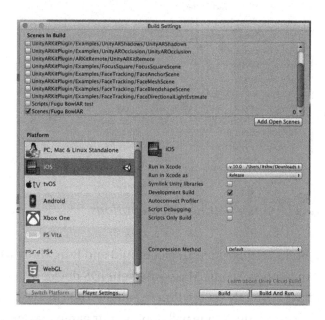

Figure 7-26. *The Build Settings Menu*

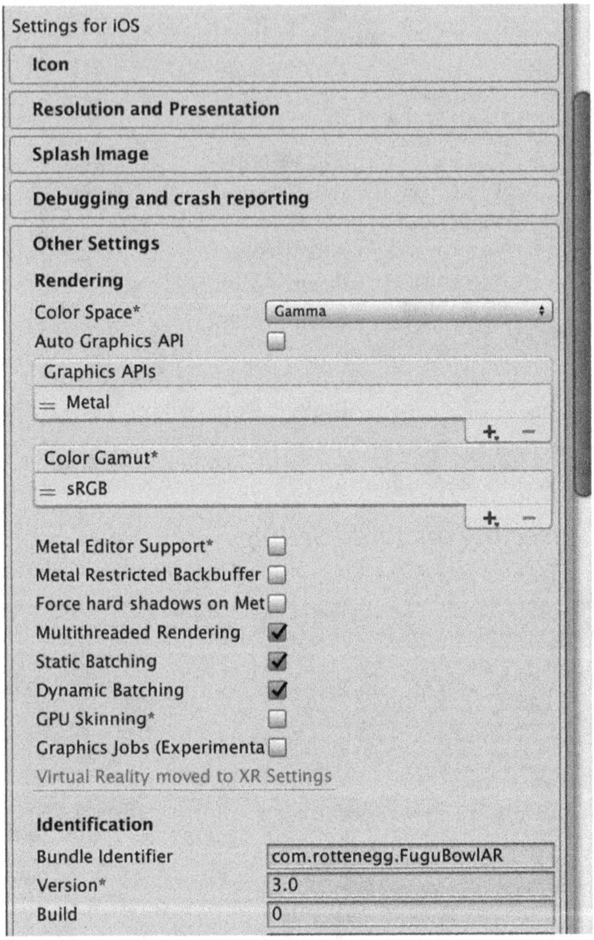

Settings for iOS

Icon

Resolution and Presentation

Splash Image

Debugging and crash reporting

Other Settings

Rendering

Color Space* | Gamma   ⬍ |

Auto Graphics API   ☐

Graphics APIs

☰ Metal

                                                                    +̣ −

Color Gamut*

☰ sRGB

                                                                    +̣ −

Metal Editor Support*   ☐
Metal Restricted Backbuffer   ☐
Force hard shadows on Met   ☐
Multithreaded Rendering   ☑
Static Batching   ☑
Dynamic Batching   ☑
GPU Skinning*   ☐
Graphics Jobs (Experimenta   ☐
Virtual Reality moved to XR Settings

Identification

Bundle Identifier | com.rottenegg.FuguBowlAR |
Version* | 3.0 |
Build | 0 |

Figure 7-27. *The Other Settings Menu options*

From the Build Settings menu, select Build and Run. Unity will compile the code and then open Xcode. Make sure your iOS device is connected and that you have correctly set the Provisioning Profile in Xcode. If everything is set correctly, Xcode will deploy your game to your iOS device, and you can test the build.

Bringing Balance to the Force

When we tested our game in the Game view, we found that the BowlingBall GameObject was probably going a bit too fast. If you were able to test the game on your iOS device, you probably felt that we had a similar situation. The process of making a game fair or balanced is not easy; it requires a lot of planning and testing. In our game we have the BowlingBall GameObject set at 5 m/h. As you might imagine, the average bowler is unlikely to be able to bowl a bowling ball at 5 m/h. However, as this is a game, we have some latitude and creative license. But, we don't want to make the game too hard or too easy. Finding this balance is challenging. Like all the great cooking shows, I am going to test the settings and report on the result. However, if you want to try testing different speeds for the bowling ball, this would be a great experience. I would, however, recommend testing the game in the Game view and not deploying the build to your iOS device.

Slowing Down the Bowling Ball

There are two ways we can slow down the bowling ball. We could increase its mass (make it heavier) or we can slow down its move speed. I prefer the second option. In the Hierarchy, select the BowlingBall GameObject and in the Inspector set the Move Speed in the Player Example component to 0.5 (Figure 7-28).

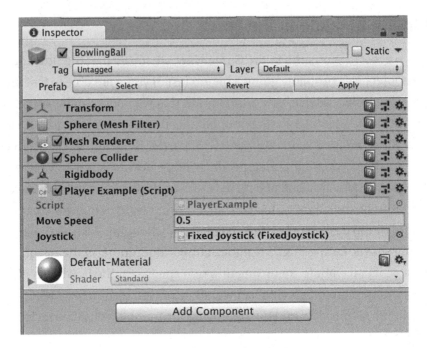

Figure 7-28. *The adjusted Move Speed settings*

I am reasonably happy with this setting, but some user testing is going to help us confirm if this speed is too slow.

Lighting

Just like we did in Chapter 4, we are going to adjust our lighting so that the lights in the game are a closer approximation to the lighting in the real world.

Turning Off the Lights

We are going to use a different light source for our App. However, for best results, let's make sure we have turned off all the lights in the scene.

From the Main Menu, select Window ➤ Lighting ➤ Settings (Figure 7-29).

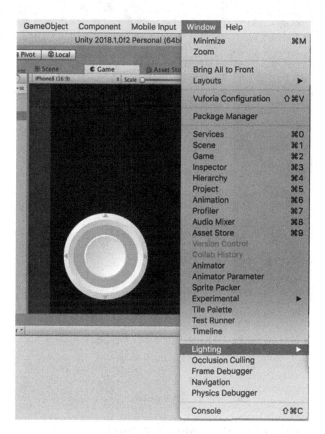

Figure 7-29. *Selecting the Lighting Settings*

In the Lighting Settings, in the Environment settings, change the Intensity Multiplier to zero. In the Mixed Lighting settings, uncheck the Baked Illumination settings (Figure 7-30).

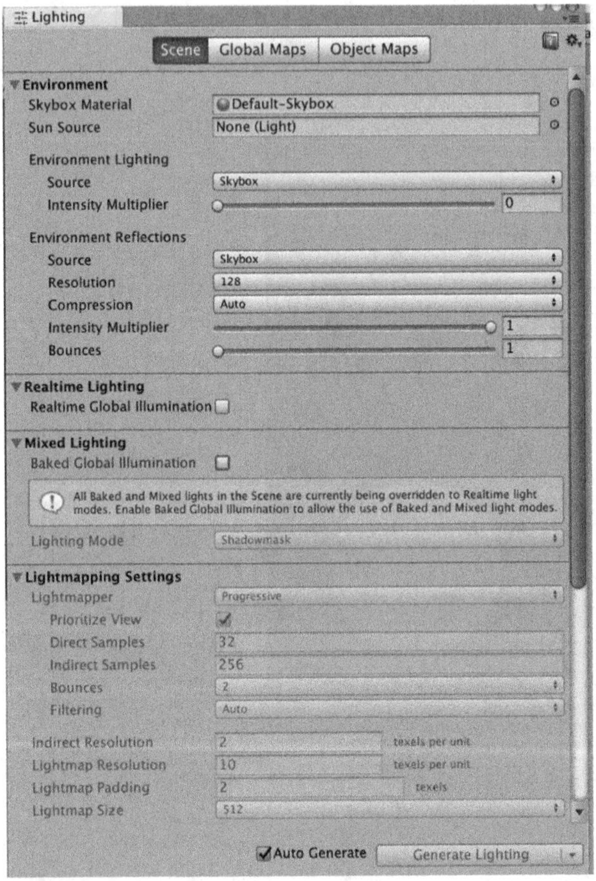

Figure 7-30. Changing the Lighting Settings

Now select the Directional Light and in the Inspector, change the color to white. And type in the RGB or HSV values of the color you want in the properties box (Figure 7-31).

Figure 7-31. *Typing in the color properties*

Setting the Ambient Light Source

Now we can set the ambient light source. With the Directional Light selected, select the Add Component button and search for ambient (Figure 7-32).

Figure 7-32. *Searching for the Unity AR Ambient*

You will see that the Unity ARKit has also included a script called
Unity AR Ambient. Select this script to add it to our Directional Light
(Figure 7-33).

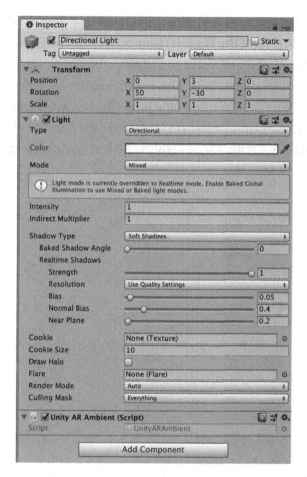

Figure 7-33. The Unity AR Ambient script added to the Directional Light

Summary

In this chapter, we added the Plane Detection and Point Clouds to our Game. We also improved the lighting to make the lighting in the game look closer to the lighting in the real world. In our next chapter, we will look at adding Sound to our game.

The more experienced developers that read this chapter will probably realize that we still have the Plane(t) GameObject in the Game. If we remove the Plane(t) GameObject completely, the BowlingBall and the Bowling_Pin will keep on falling. This is because these GameObjects are instantiating before the Created Plane is. In Chapter 8, we will cover how to instantiate these GameObjects in Unity after the Created Planes are created. For now, we have a reasonably solid test environment.

CHAPTER 8

Final Steps

In the previous chapter, we found that in order to stop the bowling ball and pin to stop falling through our generated plane, we needed to keep the Plane(t) GameObject in the scene. The reason for this is that Unity creates (or instantiates) the bowling ball and pins GameObjects before generating the generated plane. In this chapter, we are going to make some changes to our project to be able to do this

Creating Prefabs

The first step we need to take is to change our BowlingBall and Bowling_Pin GameObjects into prefabs. To do this, we need to create a Prefabs subfolder in the Assets folder. To do this, select the Assets folder in the Project Tab and right-click and select Create Folder (Figure 8-1).

© Allan Fowler 2019
A. Fowler, *Beginning iOS AR Game Development*,
https://doi.org/10.1007/978-1-4842-3618-5_8

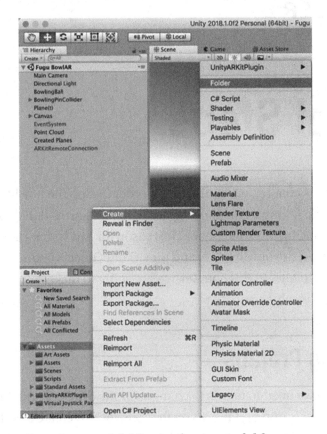

Figure 8-1. *Creating a subfolder in the Assets folder*

With the new subfolder selected, rename this to Prefabs (Figure 8-2).

Figure 8-2. *Creating a Prefabs folder*

First, I am going to rename my BowlingPinCollider GameObject to BowlingPin. To do this in the Hierarchy tab, select the BowlingPinCollider GameObject and right-click the game object and select Rename (you can also select the GameObject in the Hierarchy and then left click the file name). Now rename this file BowlingPin. This will not only keep our file-naming convention consistent, but it will also help in identifying the prefab when it is created.

Now in the Hierarchy tab, select the BowlingBall and BowlingPin GameObjects and drag these to the Prefabs folder (Figure 8-3).

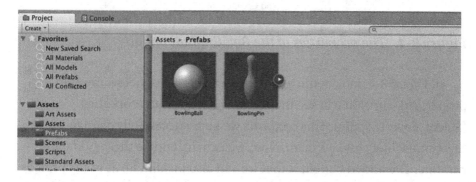

Figure 8-3. *The BowlingBall and Bowling Pin prefabs*

Now Unity has nicely converted these GameObjects to Prefabs, and now we can include them to instantiate these newly created assets at runtime. To check if these assets are now prefabs, select the BowlingPin in the Hierarchy and in the Inspector, you will see that the properties have changed (Figure 8-4).

Figure 8-4. *The properties of the BowlingBall prefab*

In Figure 8-4, look at the top of the Inspector (just below the Tag properties), and you will see that we now have Prefab Properties (Select, Revert, Apply). This confirms we have successfully changed this GameObject into a Prefab. Now, we can instantiate these prefabs at runtime. The added benefit is that we can also instantiate as many prefabs as we wish. To instantiate these game objects at runtime, we are going to need to create some code.

Adding More Bowling Pins

The first step is that we are going to add more bowling pins. To do this, we are going to update our BowlingPin Prefab. In the Hierarchy, select the Bowling_Pin GameObject and duplicate it nine times. Now we are going to rename these duplicates and transform their starting position. If you look in the Scene view or the Game View, you will note that all of the copies we made are nicely positioned at the same transform position. While this might be great for the player, we want to make this a little more challenging.

While there are correct dimensions for setting the placement for the Pin Rack, we are going to place the pins in an inverted triangle but will add a bit of artistic flair to our design.

In the Hierarchy, select the first Bowling_Pin GameObject and rename this BowlingPin 5, and in the Inspector on the Prefab settings, select Apply. Although not completely necessary in this instance, we are going to make changes to all of the Bowling_Pin GameObject's, so it is good practice to do this on all of them.

In the Hierarchy, select the second Bowling Pin GameObject and rename it BowlingPin 4. Now in the Inspector set the X transform position to -1.12 and then select Apply to apply all the changes to this Prefab. We will follow the same steps for the remaining Bowling Pins. However, to save repeating these steps on every Pin, I have summarized them in Table 8-1. When completed, you should have a similar view to what I have in Figure 8-5.

Table 8-1. *BowlingPin Settings*

BowlingPin Number	X	Y	Z
BowlingPin 1	−2.40	0	0
BowlingPin 2	−0.50	0	−1.24
BowlingPin 3	0.50	0	−1.24
BowlingPin 4	−1.12	0	0
BowlingPin 5	0	0	0
BowlingPin 6	1.12	0	0
BowlingPin 7	1.72	0	1.12
BowlingPin 8	0.60	0	1.12
BowlingPin 9	0.60	0	1.12
BowlingPin 10	−2.40	0	1.12

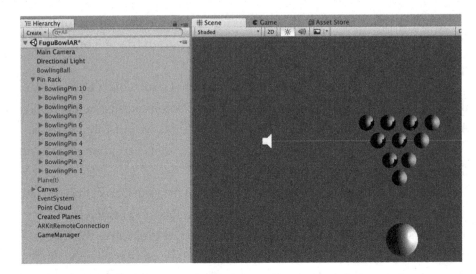

Figure 8-5. *The final Pin Rack view*

For the final touch, rename the Parent BowlingPin GameObject to Pin Rack (which is technically the correct term for our inverted triangle of Bowling Pins).

Instantiating GameObjects at Runtime

As we are going to instantiate the BowlingBall and BowlingPin Prefabs at runtime, we can disable the relevant assets in the Hierarchy. Select the BowlingBall GameObject and in the Inspector, deselect the check box next to the name of the Prefab (Figure 8-6).

Figure 8-6. *Deselecting the BowlingBall from the Scene*

You will note that that the BowlingBall Prefab is no longer visible in the Scene view. Repeat this same step for the Pin Rack.

Creating an Instantiate_GameObjects Script

In case, you might have forgotten how to create a script, I'm going to repeat these steps here. If you already know, then feel free to skip the next few paragraphs.

In the Project view, select the Scripts folder and right-click and select Create ➤ C# Script (Figure 8-7).

Figure 8-7. Creating a C# Script

With the new Script selected, rename this script Instantiate_ GameObjects (Figure 8-8).

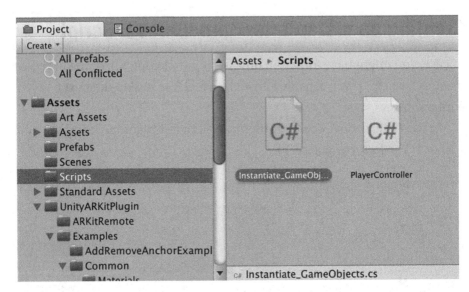

Figure 8-8. *The Instantiate_GameObjects Script file in the Scripts folder*

Now we are ready to enter our script for instantiating our Prefabs in the game at runtime. Double-click the new Instantiate_GameObjects script file we just created an in your IDE, and enter the code in Listing 8-1.

Listing 8-1. The Instantiate_GameObjects script

```csharp
using System.Collections;
using System.Collections.Generic;
using UnityEngine;

public class Instantiate_GameObjects : MonoBehaviour
{
    public GameObject bowlingBallPrefab;    //Used to store the
    bowling ball prefab and create an object based on that.
```

```csharp
public GameObject bowlingPinPrefab;     //Used to store the
bowling pin prefab and create an object based on that.

public Transform terrain; //Here just to easily double
check if we are finding the correct plane object.

public bool once = false;

// Update is called once per frame
void LateUpdate()
{
    //Look for a plane with the tag "Terrain" that will
      be generated based off another script and a prefab
      attached to it.
    terrain = GameObject.FindWithTag("Terrain").transform;
    if (once && (terrain != null))
    {
        once = false;
        InstantiateGameObjects(terrain.position);
    }
}

//Create a Bowling Ball and Pin Rack slightly above the
  plane/terrain/bowling lane.
//Called from the ARGeneratePlane script, so that
  immediately after the plane is created, the game objects
  are too with minimal resource usage.

public void InstantiateGameObjects(Vector3 plane)
{
    once = false;

    plane.y += 0.5f;
    //Make sure that the objects appear above the plane.
```

```
//Make sure the the objects appear towards the middle
  of the plane.
if(plane.x >= 0)
{
    plane.x += 2;
}
else
{
    plane.x += -2;
}

Instantiate(bowlingBallPrefab, plane, Quaternion.
identity);  //Create the Pin Rack

    }
}
```

Disabling a GameObject from the Scene

Just in case you're not sure how to disable a GameObject, select the Plane(t)
GameObject in the Hierarchy, and in the Inspector, deselect it by clicking the
check box just next to the name of the GameObject (Figure 8-9).

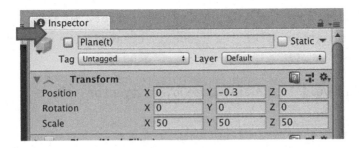

Figure 8-9. A disabled GameObject

Creating a Game Manager

We are now going to create a Game Manager. Game Managers are great places to hold assets like Scoring Systems, Audio managers, and they will be a good place to contain the Instantiate_GameObjects script we created.

In the Hierarchy, create an Empty GameObject and name it GameManager. From the Scripts Folder in the Project view, drag the Instantiate_GameObjects script onto this GameObject (Figure 8-10).

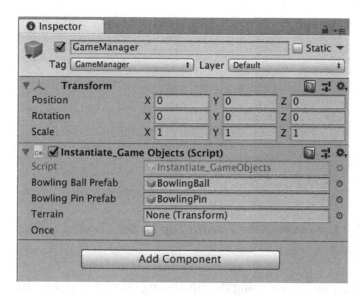

Figure 8-10. *The GameManager with the Instantiate_GameObjects script*

In Figure 8-10, I have added the BowlingBall and the BowlingPin Prefab to the GameManager.

FindWithTag

The astute reader will notice that in our Instantiate_GameObjects Script, we referred to the FindWithTag function. We need to update our Created Planes GameObject to add this tag.

In the Hierarchy, select the Created Planes GameObject and in the Inspector, select the drop-down menu of the Tag Properties and Select the Tag Terrain (Figure 8-11).

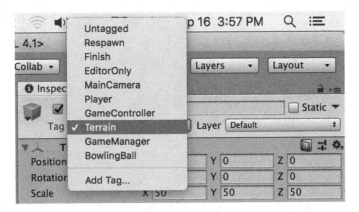

Figure 8-11. *Selecting the Terrain Tag for the Created Planes GameObject*

As we are no longer using the Hit Testing Component, we can disable this (Figure 8-12).

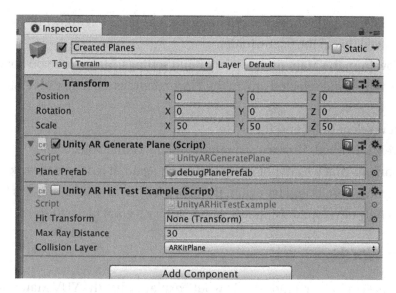

Figure 8-12. *The Created Planes GameObject settings*

For our game, we really don't need the Point Clouds, so I'm going to also disable them from the scene.

Now would be a good time to save our game.

Testing

In the world of game development (and application development), we can't avoid testing and retesting. However, this time, I am going to build and try to run my awesome game on my device. The first thing we need to do is disable the ARKitRemote GameObject in the scene. I'm not going to remove it just yet, as I feel we might have some more testing and development to do.

In the Hierarchy, select the ARKitRemote Game Object and deselect it.

Now would be a good time to save our game. I have decided to use version control for my scene file name. This way, if anything goes wrong, I can go back to the scene that worked. Therefore, from the menu, I selected

File ➤ Save As and I choose to call my Scene file name FuguBowlAR Test, and I saved this in the Scene folder.

Now from the Main menu, select Build settings. Make sure you have the current scene selected and in the Player Settings, change the version number.

Now select Build and Run.

Well, it worked. Now we can remove all the GameObjects and components that we are not using and test it again. If it does not work, check your settings and try again. It worked for me, and I'll admit, it's far from a fully developed shippable game, but it's a great place to start.

Final Words

In an earlier chapter, I indicated I would explain what the YUV Material does in the properties box of the Clear Material settings in the Unity AR Video Script. The YUV Material is a shader that fills the background buffer with real-world video. In this case, we are using the shader to "project" real-world video from the camera onto the game. YUV is a color-encoding system typically used as part of a color image pipeline. It encodes a color image or video taking human perception into account. For a detailed explanation of the YUV color-encoding system, there is a very good explanation here: `https://docs.microsoft.com/en-us/windows/desktop/medfound/about-yuv-video`.

There is a lot more to game development than what we covered in this book. The next step would be adding a user interface, and when fully polished, we might want to publish our game on the Asset Store. There are already a number of great books and tutorials on publishing on the Asset Store (for example: `https://unity3d.com/learn/tutorials/topics/mobile-touch/how-submit-ios-app-store-overview`, or `https://developer.apple.com/app-store/resources/`). I recommend that you check these resources out and hope you will let me know when you have published your AR game. Ganbatte kudasai (good luck)!

Summary

In this chapter, we converted our two GameObjects into prefabs. Then we created and updated our BowlingBall Prefab. We then added a script to Instantiate the GameManager Script that will add these prefabs to the game at runtime.

Index

© Allan Fowler 2019
A. Fowler, *Beginning iOS AR Game Development*,
https://doi.org/10.1007/978-1-4842-3618-5

V, W, X, Y, Z

Printed in the United States
By Bookmasters